RISEN INDEED

Also published by D.L.T.

May One Believe – in Russia?
(ed. Michael Bourdeaux and Michael Rowe)

RISEN INDEED
Lessons in Faith from the USSR

Michael Bourdeaux

Foreword by
Bishop Donald Coggan

KESTON BOOK NO. 16

Darton, Longman and Todd
London

St Vladimir's Seminary Press
Crestwood, New York 10707
1983

First published in 1983 by
Darton, Longman and Todd Ltd
89 Lillie Road, London SW6 1UD
and
St Vladimir's Seminary Press
575 Scarsdale Road
Crestwood, New York 10707

ISBN 0 232 51506 9 (DLT)
ISBN 0–88141–021–7 (SVS Press)

Phototypeset by Input Typesetting Ltd, London SW19 8DR
Printed in Great Britain by The Anchor Press Ltd
and bound by Wm Brendon & Son Ltd
both of Tiptree, Essex

To Lorna

Contents

Foreword

I have found this an informative and moving book, and I hope it will be widely read.

People like ourselves, who live in countries where there is complete freedom of religion, freedom of expression and lack of persecution, find it hard to imagine what life is like for great numbers of Christians and others who believe that those things matter but who live under regimes which hate and despise them.

Some of us prefer not to hear about such situations – life is more comfortable if we close our ears. Others do not know where to get reliable information – 'you can't believe everything the papers tell you'.

This little book should serve to stab awake the consciences of the comfortable. It will serve to provide completely reliable information for those who want to know what is going on in modern Russia – for facts from Keston College can be trusted.

It will do more, if it does for others what it has done for me. It will provide a very humbling experience as one reads stories of 'martyrdom' in the sense of immensely costly witness to the truth; and it will provide a strong injection of hope as one watches the power of love over hate, and of unity through the experience of Christ's presence.

Michael Bourdeaux's deepest wish will be granted if the reading of his book arouses continuing prayer for those who suffer in exile, prison, or 'remedial' psychiatric hospitals.

Donald Coggan

Acknowledgements

The initial stimulus for this book came from Canon Colin Semper who invited me to state the relevance of the Russian Christian experience for us in a Radio 4 Lent Lecture in 1980. I have incorporated some material from the resulting script.

My main quarry of material for this volume lay close to hand: the journal of Keston College, *Religion in Communist Lands*. Over the years it has published an abundance of spiritual writing from the Soviet Union which testifies to the still depths of faith beneath turbulent surface water.

I am grateful to Alexander Solzhenitsyn, the Bodley Head and Farrar, Straus and Giroux for permission to quote the lengthy extract from *August 1914* on pp. 55–7. English translation copyright © 1972 by Michael Glenny.

I hope that readers who are stimulated by this book may support the work of Keston College and subscribe to its publications. This work is dependent entirely on private donations.

My thanks are due to Sir John Lawrence, Dr Philip Walters, Mavis King, Alyona Kojevnikov and Paul Lucey, who read the manuscript and made many valuable suggestions. Thanks also to my wife, who typed it.

Michael Bourdeaux
Keston College, Keston, Kent, England

INTRODUCTION

A Few Pages of Autobiography

God's signature is on the small events of this world just as indelibly as on the large. His two direct interventions into my life when he wrested the steering wheel from my grasp to set me on a new course could hardly have been in greater contrast. The first was an insignificant ailment, cleared up in a few days, without which I would probably never have learned a word of Russian. The second was a coincidence, a miracle so much against the odds that in comparison to win a million on the pools would seem commonplace. After all, in gambling someone has to win, even if it is only the bookmaker, while what happened to me in Moscow in 1964 was so improbable that no fiction writer would dare invent such an episode.

I have suffered from toothache only twice. The first time was when I was eighteen and the painful, swollen abscess seemed to have appeared exactly at the right time to give me a few welcome extra days at home.

I had just completed the first eight weeks of my National Service, the 'square-bashing' period, as we called it, following which all recruits were granted a long weekend at home. I had scarcely ever had a day's illness in my life, but my overnight journey on the train from Hednesford in Staffordshire to Cornwall was made sleepless by growing agony from a swelling gum. My dentist had to extract the molar even before I sat in my favourite armchair in the pleasant house in the country to which my parents had just moved. The dentist said the doctor must put me on a course of antibiotics. The doctor said I should have a week at home, the most welcome news there could possibly be after the rigours of the previous two months.

1

Returning to camp a week late, I felt rather pleased at the turn of events, considering one tooth a small price to pay for the luxury which had come my way. My complacency was immediately shattered. The next major event in the sequence of Air Force life for the national serviceman was 'posting': the moment at which the bureaucracy grouped every recruit into one of about eight trades which provided employment for the next twenty-two months.

I imagined I would be posted a week late. I was on a special list. As a person who had had a training – and I must say an excellent one – in the Modern Language Sixth at Truro School, I had been singled out by the system as an interpreter to go to West Germany and help our troops stationed there. There was an examination of about O-level standard to pass first and I had an A-level, with a place to read French and German at Oxford after National Service.

The only problem was that the exam had already taken place. In the first real shock of my whole life, I discovered that in my absence the original posting had been cancelled and I was instead assigned to 'general office duties' – kindling unwilling fires, making tea and scrubbing floors.

I saw the officer of my section. No, nothing could be done, he said. The system was fixed, the chosen interpreters from my unit had already left for Germany for a spell of training in the country. I did understand, didn't I, that opportunities for national servicemen were very limited and that I might have been put down for far less pleasant duties in the cook-house. Please would I be on duty in the unit office first thing next day. Horrified, I asked whether there was any forum for appeal against posting. Putting on a stiff face, the officer said there was, but he felt it his duty to warn me that the consequences of stepping out of line were not always pleasant. However, if I insisted he would arrange an interview with the commanding officer. Meanwhile, my general duties would begin. . . .

I did insist. The commanding officer turned out to be a real gentleman who dispelled my nerves at once, showing immediate concern for the plight I was in. However, he said solemnly, the system was too bureaucratic for him to be able to do anything. The country was still insisting on universal recruitment of young men, without really considering the tiny range of worthwhile openings for those in for two years. If I would like to take on a short-service commission for three years, he could immediately reopen the file. End of conversation. Should I drink the last half of the cup of tea he had so kindly provided? I just did not know the etiquette. I took one compromise sip in silence and shuffled my chair to stand up.

'Mm. Just a moment, Bourdeaux. Finish your tea. I really do feel you've had a raw deal, you know. What was that circular which came around last week? No, I can't see it here. . . .' He shuffled through the papers on his desk. My tea was gone. 'Something about languages.' The three words were mumbled, but they broke the silence. Was there a glimmer of hope? 'Oh, yes, here it is. Russian. That's what was on my mind. Yes, the Government has recently started training Russian linguists to help our boys who may have to fight Jo Stalin and the Russkis in the next war. Doesn't give details of when the courses start. Wait a minute.' He lifted the telephone. 'Give me the Records Office at Gloucester, please. . . . Hello. Commanding Officer of Hednesford here. Please give me the section dealing with my postings. I've got a young man here, missed his German posting. Tell me about the Russian course. . . . Vacancies in two months? Put Bourdeaux on it, please.' Putting the phone down, he said, 'Right, you will go to Coulsdon in Surrey in two months, then on to Cambridge for the highest level of interpreters' course if you pass the initial exam. Better make sure you don't fail. Go and work in the library for the next few weeks. See if there's a Russian book in the *Teach Yourself* series and get started. I'll test you in a month!'

I never saw the Group Captain again. I cannot remember his name, but I shall never forget him.

The second incident occurred twelve years later, in 1964. I had already completed university degrees in Russian and French and later Theology. I had happened to be free at exactly the right time to take advantage of the first ever exchange of British students for a year to a Soviet University (1959–60). In Moscow I had made Russian friends, Christian and atheist, and felt sure that in a very real sense my life was following a definite direction. Having been ordained as a priest in the Anglican Church after my return from Moscow, I knew inside that I should somehow be serving the Church overseas, using my languages in the service of God, rather than preparing for a lifetime of pastoral work in Britain. Obviously my special area of interest was Eastern Europe, not the conventional missionary field. I had become a curate in a North London parish. I had sketched out my Soviet experiences into a draft of what eventually became my first book, *Opium of the People*, and had had an article published in *The Observer*.

Publishers were not interested in the book – 'Danger of rocking the boat', said one Christian editor. 'Your views don't accord with those who are trying to establish good relations between the Anglican and Russian Orthodox Churches, and in any case all this talk of persecution can only harm Christians in the Soviet Union itself, even if it were true.'

As it went from publisher to publisher (twelve altogether) the manuscript became more dog-eared and out of date. I had been happy in my first three years as a curate and by now had a wife and infant daughter for whom I had to plan also. In the fourth year the horizons of the parish seemed to become constricting. Those cherished words of Milton came insistently into my mind:

> And that one talent which is death to hide,
> Lodged with me useless.

Then out of the blue came a letter from Faber and Faber. They could not publish the book in its present form, but they liked its style and it was on a subject which was hardly represented on the current bookshelves of libraries. If I could rewrite it completely, working current information into the pattern of my own experience in the Soviet Union, then they might. . . .

This was not a contract, but it was a tremendous challenge, as I had found interest from one of the best secular publishing houses after having exhausted all the main religious ones.

Despite the disparaging words of the Christian editor, there was serious, perhaps increasing, persecution of the Church in the Soviet Union. Of that I was sure. But it was virtually impossible to uncover details of it. I had gone to Moscow for a second visit, three weeks as an interpreter at the British Exhibition in 1961, but had learned scarcely anything new. People were as terrified to talk as they had been during my student year. Stalin had been dead for less than a decade still. Now at the beginning of 1964 I had no money to go to Moscow again and even if I had there was no guarantee the expense would be justified.

As I was thinking all this through, God's timing was perfect once again. An envelope arrived containing a short duplicated letter on green paper, an English translation of a letter from a Ukrainian Christian. It was accompanied by a note from my old friend and teacher at Oxford, the late Dr Nicholas Zernov. He said a document had come to him from a school-teacher friend in Paris, a girl of Russian origin who had recently been in Moscow. There she had met some Orthodox Christians from the distant west of the Soviet Union who had given her an appeal to the outside world, begging people to intervene with the Soviet Government and prevent the imminent closure of the Pochaev Monastery, one of the greatest Christian shrines of the country. Dr Zernov could not vouch for the authenticity of the letter, nor did he know whether it should be publicized, but he had translated it so that at least it could be shown privately to some interested people.

The appeal recounted heartbreaking persecutions: monks beaten up by the KGB, subjected to humiliating medical examinations, thrown out on to the streets; if they came back into their quarters from which the local authorities were trying to evict them, they were rounded up, pushed into lorries, taken hundreds of kilometres into the countryside, far from the nearest house, and just dumped. The authors wrote with absolute simplicity, just listing the facts to which they claimed to be eyewitnesses. There were two names at the end, Varavva and Pronina, surnames unadorned even by an initial.

Moved by what I read, I had the gut feeling that I was for the first time in my life hearing the true voices of the persecuted Church. But what should I do? With whom should I talk? Now in the 1980s there are reported to be as many as one hundred and fifty missionary societies, large and small, setting out in some way to help Christians in Eastern Europe. But except for a handful, these are all of very recent provenance. The two or three which did already exist (the Slavic Gospel Association in Chicago, Slaviska Missionen in Stockholm, Aid to the Church in Nccd in Belgium) had so little work in Britain that their existence was unknown to me.

If the words of the document were true, then the persecution had become much worse, far more physical and brutal, than I had imagined. There was clearly more to do than just to write. I really had to become more personally involved and see whether there was something I could actively do to help. It was now a priority to return to the Soviet Union.

1964 provided not one but two opportunities. First in April I managed to obtain a very cheap trip with a group of teachers. On the few occasions that I could break free from the group, conversations were inhibited by the all-pervading fear. I talked to some warm and wonderful people, but on new information my sheet of paper remained blank. Hardly was I back from this than an invitation came to accompany a group of Americans as leader – a free trip and an offer I could not refuse. It was on this second visit in August that God wrenched the steering wheel out of my grasp.

On my first evening in Moscow I went to see some old

6

friends. They were delighted to see me unexpectedly a second time that year and immediately began answering the questions I had put four months previously. 'It's providential you've come back again. The persecution has become so much worse since you were last here in April. By then we had heard rumours that it was very bad in the provinces, but now it's started to affect us right here in Moscow. Do you know that Church of St Peter and St Paul, that beautiful one standing on its own in the centre of a square? Well, they demolished it last week, despite protests. A ring of people standing round it after the authorities had closed it didn't stop the soldiers moving in, fixing a dynamite charge and detonating it. You'd better go and see for yourself.'

I took a taxi at once, so that I could be there in order to catch the last of the daylight. There were several churches of St Peter and Paul in Moscow, but my friends had told me the exact location of this one. I stopped the taxi short of the square, so that no suspicions should be aroused, and I walked on alone. From my student days I remembered the beautiful church with its one central large and four smaller surrounding cupolas. But now the great square was empty, except for a circular wooden fence about twelve feet high, totally blocking any view of what lay inside it. I was afraid to go too close, feeling sure that the square must be under constant observation. From a slight hill up one side street I could just see some twisted metal on top of a pile of masonry, the remains of what had been the crosses on the cupolas. My attention was attracted by two dumpy black figures across the road. Standing right by the fence, one was trying to hoist the other up by her elbows to peer in or over – not very successfully, I guessed, in view of the girth and short stature of both. But now I could see the point of the exercise. There was a chink between two of the boards forming the fence and this became broader the higher it went.

I must talk to these women, I said to myself; they could tell me more details of what has happened. I waited until they had left the square, followed them quietly for a hundred yards, caught up with them and said, '*Skazhitye, pozhaluista.* . . . Tell me, please, do you know what's happened here?'

They jumped back, terrified as I thought. 'Who are you?'

I did not know what to say, but I answered: 'I'm a foreigner, just come to find out more about the Church here in the Soviet Union – but if you're afraid to talk to me I'll leave you alone.'

'No you won't. You're a foreigner? We need you.' As she said this, one of them put her hand forward and placed it firmly on my shoulder. 'Come with us, we need to talk to you.'

I followed discreetly behind them, not talking any more for fear of attracting attention. We walked, boarded a bus, then a tram. We were on the very edge of Moscow, where country villages, their little wooden houses nestling among the trees, were already being consumed by the square solid blocks of Khrushchev's new Moscow.

Ahead of me, the two women walked into an old wooden building and straight up a flight of stairs, where there was another woman just like them waiting.

'See what God has brought us – a young man from abroad', said one.

'Yes, but who are you really?', asked the other who had come in with me.

'I'm an Englishman. I used to study at Moscow University. I met many Christians here. Then recently I heard that the persecution of the Church was getting worse in the Soviet Union. I decided I must come back to see if this were true and whether I could do anything at all to help my Christian friends.'

'Wonderful, wonderful . . . but why precisely did you come?', asked the third, the woman whose flat this was.

'I received a document. . . .'

'What document?'

'It was from Ukraine, from Pochaev, sent via a schoolteacher from Paris.'

'Who wrote it?'

'Two women. . . .'

'What were their names?'

'Mm . . . Varavva and – oh, yes – Pronina.'

Suddenly the silence was total. I wondered if I'd said something wrong. Then a deep sob from the third woman. 'My guests . . . this is Feodosia Varavva.'

'Yes, I wrote that appeal. This is Pronina who signed it, too.'

'When we'd written it we came to Moscow, nearly 1,300 kilometres, to find a foreigner. We searched for days unsuccessfully, but eventually we met a French school-teacher who happened to speak Russian. She took the letter for us.'

'I never met her', I said, 'but I got it through a friend a few weeks later. I came back to find out more.'

'It was over six months ago that we last came to Moscow. But since then so much has happened. Things have got much worse. They're putting our monks into psychiatric prisons. We wrote several new documents and so did the monks themselves. We arrived here this afternoon to look for another foreigner, but before we had time to start our search, our friend here sent us out to see the terrible things which have been happening in Moscow itself. That's where we met you.'

From that moment the direction of my life was set. I could see that I had to find some way of serving the persecuted Church full time. As there were no existing organizations I knew doing this, it would mean giving up personal security and branching out on my own. Perhaps thirty was the right age for this, yet my responsibility to provide for my family was daunting. I felt totally impotent then to respond to the hand on my shoulder, to the commission, 'We need you'. How could I, a lone voice who scarcely had a voice, respond to the needs of millions of suffering Christians? Yet I could never even contemplate ignoring such a call.

Those voices are still in my head today as I write these words, aiming now to set down a distillation of what I have personally learned from my experience of the Church in the USSR over the past twenty years. While I was writing the first draft of this very page the news came through from Moscow (28 August 1980) of the trial of Father Gleb Yakunin, one of the saints of our age. A ten-year sentence on a totally innocent man. Again, the feeling of impotence. Has anything really been achieved in the cause of religious liberty in the intervening years? Perhaps not much. There are a few encouraging signs, but they are widely scattered. We do, however, now have a Keston College to relay the news to the world by telex. Building this up has been my work of the last decade. We started with nothing but a little faith and my personal archives. Now we have highly qualified full-time research workers and excellent sources of information.

The news of Father Gleb's arrest came through from Moscow by telephone within an hour after the pronouncement of the sentence, but shortly after this the telephone was cut off, later to be replaced by another link. Some will pray and this will be a true source of strength to Father Gleb during the bitter years of separation from his family which he is now undergoing. But, with few exceptions, church leaders worldwide have predictably failed to encourage action and sacrifice from us on his behalf.

PART I

Revival

1

The Seed of the Church

After twenty years studying and experiencing the life of the Church in the Soviet Union at first hand, it is time for me to ask myself why it is important for every one to know about it and what are the essential lessons it has to teach the world.

Suffering lies at the heart of the gospel. Without the crucifixion there can be no resurrection. Yet if you look around the western democracies today you will scarcely anywhere find even a self-sacrificing church, let alone a suffering one. The Churches of the Soviet Union, whether one looks at Orthodox, Protestants or Catholics, are all persecuted. Therefore, whatever their theological differences (and these are proving to be so much less important than what they share, even if they are not fully aware of this yet), they are all closer to the New Testament than we are. No one ever expressed this more succinctly than Tertullian when, looking back over two centuries of persecution and with one more to go before the Roman Empire was to adopt Christianity, he wrote: 'The more you mow us down, the more we grow; the seed is the blood of Christians.'

Turned into its popular form, 'The blood of the martyrs is the seed of the Church', this text rings out as the motto of the Church in the Soviet Union (I avoid saying 'the Russian Church', because this excludes the millions belonging to minority nationalities such as Lithuanians and Ukrainians who also share in this persecution). Though the world at large still ignores the testimony of the Church under communism, the day cannot now be far away when lessons will be learned and great inspiration will flow back from the persecuted Churches to the privileged ones to revitalize them. It is a miracle that

13

this revival has begun in the Soviet Union itself and has reached a climax already in Poland, but it is a miracle which has ample historical precedent and therefore should not stun people with amazement in the way it does when they hear about it for the first time.

It is not a fair assessment – indeed, it is a communist slander assiduously propagated – to claim that the Russian Orthodox Church before the Revolution of 1917 was totally corrupt and ripe for persecution. There was much wrong with it, but how many of our Churches today are blameless? There was also much that was good in it. There was the timeless tradition of holy men, the *startsy*, who still exist today. It was active in education. There was a strong reforming element within it. The henchmen first of Lenin then of Stalin tried to liquidate the good even more than the bad.

It was this first persecution, begun immediately after the Revolution, perhaps the worst in numbers of Christians the world has ever known, that put the seal of martyrdom on the Russian Orthodox Church of the twentieth century. There were no half measures. This was the death of a Church. Tens of thousands of priests and monks and almost all the bishops were imprisoned or exiled to Siberia, where they died in untold numbers. Their flocks were scattered, very many being themselves exiled. Almost all the churches closed and many were physically destroyed. Thus not only were believers denied access to objects of popular devotion, especially ikons, which were confiscated from churches and often even from private homes; they also lost any possibility of seeing their children educated as Christians, as every form of religious education, public and private, was banned. The theological seminaries and monasteries were abolished. The printing of Christian literature ceased. The four bishops who remained at liberty did the regime's bidding and had nothing to administer, no proper diocese, not even a central office ('Patriarchate', as it now is). No recitation of facts and figures could ever convey the feeling of devastation which overwhelmed the Russian Church at this period. Alexander Solzhenitsyn's *Gu-

lag Archipelago, a work of literature as well as of history, comes closest to doing so, while there are now Christian memoirs which have been circulated or concealed for two generations in manuscript and are at last emerging to give us an understanding of how the roots of the present revival must be sought in the apparent liquidation of the Church fifty years earlier.

The most accessible of these is *The Unknown Homeland*, published first in English in 1978 and as yet in no other language. Even in Britain it has received virtually no recognition, though it is a magnificent work of literature, a direct descendant of the classics of the nineteenth century. Shortly after his enthronement, the Archbishop of Canterbury, Dr Robert Runcie, wrote of it:

> During the days before my enthronement as Archbishop of Canterbury, I had little time for reading; but I discovered a little known spiritual classic which combined charm, readability and depth in a unique way. It was *The Unknown Homeland* and forms part of that remarkable treasure which is emerging from contemporary Russian religious experience.

The story is simple. It is the biography (written anonymously by a close relative) of an ordinary priest, Father Pavel, whose ministry spanned only two and a half decades. His early brilliance as a theologian before ordination had been dimmed by the distraction of falling in love with and marrying a beautiful, intelligent though ultimately unworthy girl. Instead of following his original calling to live in peace and monastic seclusion where he could pursue his writing, Father Pavel found himself ministering in a busy central parish in St Petersburg (later Leningrad). After the Revolution life became gradually more difficult for him and, though his wife did not abandon him, she dealt him the shattering spiritual blow of abandoning the faith to become an atheist lecturer. The net was already around him and inevitably the cord of persecution drew it tighter. Only when it finally enclosed him

15

and carried him away into prison and exile did his real ministry begin. For this, one supposes, God called Pavel in the first place.

Father Pavel lived only about three years after his arrest. Yet confined to a cell or later to a sick bed in exile, he was the source of an influence which affected all those who came into contact with him. To this small group of people he must have seemed unique, especially to the criminal, Fyodor, whom he met in prison and who soon came to offer him the unconditional devotion of his whole life. The writer thus describes the influence of Father Pavel:

> What had happened to Fyodor often happens to people, especially young people, when they have entangled themselves to the point of madness in the twisted mess of their life and then try to find a way out of this mess, deeply longing to open their heart to another human being, to empty their soul to the core and reshape it. And he had met just such a human being in prison, an exhausted, sick man, in his worn but priestly garb, with his special, bright outlook on everything, but Fyodor had known he would be going with him on the same transport, to the same village. The young man had spent the night in troubled dreams about the priest, thinking: 'Let him understand me!' And then he would retort defiantly: 'If he doesn't understand and won't listen to me – all right, I don't need him!' 'The whole truth' sounded out as an answer to his doubts; the sweet pain of repentance and the consolation that would follow filled his soul.

In fact Father Pavel was one of thousands, lay and clerical, Orthodox and Protestant (there were very few Catholics in the Soviet Union at that time before the Second World War pushed the frontiers westward), who between them preserved and purified the faith, inspiring millions to carry it on revitalized into the next generation. The writer's epitaph shows the whole process of the new life of faith being born in the midst of death:

16

The same evening, when Father Pavel's death became known, half the collective farm came to the Zakharovs' house. The priest had lived there for about four months, but for many people he had become their 'adviser', 'benefactor' and 'dear father'. . . .

So the story of the exiled pastor came to an end. . . . But though the storm blows over the new and old grave mounds, covering them with snow, though the snowstorm whirls over the distant cemetery, wrapping it in a mantle of white snow, though time goes by and the years disappear, though no one comes there any more and the small cross with its worn inscription falls off its base and collapses on to the ground . . . still the bird-cherry tree will go on arraying itself anew in its wedding colours every spring, and the path of remembrance, prayer and veneration, which leads to such graves, will never be overgrown. . . .

There is a clear link between the persecutions of the 1930s and the revival of today, with the Second World War causing a break from the old pattern of persecution. There was a new, dramatic, but short-lived hope for the Soviet Christian, associated with the German invasion. There was also a change in Soviet policy, but this, too, in its turn, proved to be fragile less than twenty years later.

The huge tracts of European Russia and of the Ukraine which fell to the Nazis witnessed a spectacular religious revival in which almost the whole population joined. As the Red Army recaptured these lands in the later phase of the war and then proceeded to push Soviet frontiers further west in the wake of the retreating Germans, the political commissars reactivated the persecutions and subdued those areas which had never been Soviet before.

Yet at the same time another policy coexisted. The office of Patriarch had been unfilled since the death of Tikhon nearly twenty years earlier. Then in September 1943 Stalin summoned Metropolitan Sergi to the Kremlin for a meeting. Though the terms of the concordat they concluded have never been published, the immediate result was that a hastily – and uncanonically – convened *sobor* (council) appointed Sergi as Patriarch. When he died the next year, there was a rather larger and more regular gathering, including guests of honour from abroad, which appointed Metropolitan Alexi as his successor. Priests emerged from the camps, churches reopened their doors, theological education resumed after a hiatus of nearly thirty years and even a tiny publishing programme began (just the single title, *Journal of the Moscow Patriarchate*). Bishops returned to dioceses which they were now permitted to administer, the Church was allowed to establish a nerve-centre, the Moscow Patriarchate, while the state demonstrated its intention of keeping control by setting up a new body, eventually known as the Council on Religious Affairs, to watch over church activities (for thirty years its charter remained secret). This new 'stability' was to be destroyed by Nikita Khrushchev soon after his accession to power in the mid-1950s.

But there was a parallel revival of a third kind, represented by the steadfastness of those bishops and clergy who would in no way compromise with the state in order to win personal liberty. One such was Bishop Afanasi of Kovrov. Among his papers after his death there was a four-page autobiographical sketch just listing the dates and places where he had been. During the years when the Church first regained its 'liberty' he was working on a night brigade in Siberian exile. 27 June 1954 was the 33rd anniversary of his consecration as bishop, during which years he had been able to serve just 33 months in his diocese. He was free but barred from office for a similar period of time, while the remaining five-sixths of his life as a bishop were divided between prison and exile. In a moving paragraph appended to this paper, the Bishop stated that the longer he had been away from his diocese, the more his people prayed for him and helped him. The proof of this was that at the beginning of his imprisonment he was receiving about thirty food parcels a year, while by 1954, his last year before release, this had risen to two hundred.

Men and women who inspire such devotion have only to be themselves to transmit the faith to the young, to a generation 'Soviet' by birth and supposedly by upbringing. They have influenced some among the younger generation who demonstrate the true beginnings of a religious revival in the Soviet Union.

It is invidious to select one individual to represent this revival. Yet I have to do so, and therefore choose Father Gleb Yakunin. By coincidence he is my exact contemporary, having been born like me in March 1934. I choose him because he is Orthodox and because he is at this moment suffering bitterly for his faith. The Baptists have received some publicity in recent years, the Orthodox not nearly enough. When Father Gleb was sentenced to ten years in August 1980 the world's press reacted as though they had never heard of him, whereas he already had behind him by then fifteen years of outstanding service in the cause of religious liberty.

He comes from a religious family, but lost his faith after the war at the age of fifteen. He yearned for an open-air life and entered a forestry institute in Irkutsk, Siberia. There he came under the influence of one of the great evangelists of the Russian Orthodox Church, Father Alexander Men, who led him back to the Church. His temporary break from it ensured that his return would be with the greater conviction. Burning with zeal, he returned to Moscow, determined to become a priest. His mother advised him to return to finish his studies, which he did, coming back to Moscow not only with a diploma, but also with a wife, Iraida, who was to stick by him through a life of great testing. It was not easy for him to enter one of the seminaries as state control over them was so rigorous, but Archbishop Leonid of Mozhaisk (now Metropolitan of Riga) helped him and he was ordained in August 1962. His wife bore him two daughters in 1964 and 1978, with a son between them in 1974.

Though for the time he became a respected parish priest, the beginning of his pastoral work exactly coincided with the period of renewed physical persecution which marked the last

19

five years of Khrushchev's period in office (1959–64). In despair at the closure once again of monasteries, churches, seminaries and the imprisonment of the faithful, he consulted with various people, particularly with his friend, Father Nikolai Eshliman, about what could be done. He was especially upset at the continuing silence of those very people, the church leaders, whose job it should have been to defend the flock. He decided to write an open letter to the Soviet Government pointing out the illegality of the persecution and to Patriarch Alexi begging for his intervention. Eleven others, it is said, originally agreed to sign with him, but gradually, because of fear for the safety of their families, all except Father Nikolai and Father Nikolai and Father Gleb changed their minds. There was, however, one Archbishop, Yermogen of Kaluga, who made similar representations at the same time.

This made the final sending of those letters in December 1965 an act of all the greater bravery. But it was the content of those documents even more than the act of sending them which marks the greatness of Father Gleb. This was the first-ever public attempt at an overall analysis of church-state relations in the Soviet Union. The legal framework held firm the detailed infilling of specific examples of lawlessness. The letters are as valid today as when they were written and they should still be on the agenda, as they have never been properly discussed either by the Soviet state or by the Moscow Patriarchate. Major international Christian conferences outside the Soviet Union have also turned their backs on them.

The reaction of Patriarch Alexi, now in his mid-eighties, was predictable. Presumably it was the hand of the Soviet state which forced the Patriarch to suspend the two priests from all duties, though he stopped short of stripping them of their priesthood; Alexi also retired Archbishop Yermogen to a monastery, a circumstance first disclosed by the two priests themselves in an appendix to their letter to the Patriarch.

Clearly in the hope that this would facilitate an eventual just outcome, Father Gleb kept to the ban, earning his living in various minor ecclesiastical functions, and also keeping silence for almost a decade from 1966.

At Easter 1975 he broke this in order to issue a stinging rebuke to the Soviet state for 'abolishing' Easter, turning the most sacred festival in the Christian calendar into a regular working day to compensate for extra commemorative secular holidays granted by the state. Now a more political note had entered into Father Gleb's writing:

> Your newspapers have made much noise over the fuel crisis in the West. But you have been struck by the very worst of all crises – a spiritual energy crisis.
>
> Your grandfathers wanted to conquer the world. Your fathers, railway engineers, built only an uphill track, and now your train has run out of fuel.
>
> So you have decided to force the Orthodox to pull your flagging train on a great festival of the Christian calendar. . . . By designating the Easter holiday as a working day you have offended the religious feelings of millions of believers.
>
> It would have been better if you had turned 1 May and 7 November (Soviet official holidays) into working days: fewer people would have been offended.
>
> This year when we are celebrating the thirtieth anniversary of victory the decent thing would have been to thank the Russian Orthodox Church for its patriotic role in the last war, a role which you yourselves acknowledge.
>
> But in a blind, feverish pursuit of economic prosperity you are offending the feelings of many, not only churchgoers.

The stir caused by this letter, printed on the front page of the London *Sunday Telegraph*, was nothing compared with an event later that year which for the first time put Father Gleb on the international Christian stage. The World Council of Churches was to hold its postponed Fifth General Assembly in Nairobi in November. In preparation for this, and now joined by a layman, Lev Regelson, Father Gleb wrote an impassioned letter to the WCC begging the whole of international Christianity as represented by the ecumenical movement for immediate and practical help for the persecuted Church in the Soviet Union. This might have brought as little public response as previous letters from Russian Christians to the WCC (though it has often made private representations to the Soviet authorities). This time, however, the letter, translated with alacrity by friends in the West, reached first the Kenyan editors of the conference newspaper which was printed daily. Unaware of the WCC reluctance to allow debate on such issues, they published it at the very outset of the assembly. This led to an unscheduled debate, a resolution passed condemning Soviet persecution of religion, a furore, rapid backtracking on a procedural issue, and then a much milder resolution not mentioning the Soviet Union at all.

After Nairobi there was a series of meetings, leading to the establishment by the WCC of a new department on human rights and religious liberty, a desk of the Churches' Commission on International Affairs.

Father Gleb immediately followed this international initiative by something even stronger at home, the founding of the Christian Committee for the Defence of Believers' Rights in December 1976. This, more than any other single activity, led to his eventual arrest three years later. The work of Father Gleb's committee was of the highest calibre. To his previous grasp of the situation of his own Church, he now added the most vigorous defence of Baptists, Pentecostals, Adventists, Catholics and even non-Christian believers. For example, he publicized the two-year sentence on the Jew, Iosif Begun, for teaching Hebrew and would undoubtedly have expanded this aspect of his work, had he been given the liberty to do so. In the first three years of its existence before disaster struck, the Christian Committee poured out an astonishing total of 417 documents, amounting in all to 2,891 pages. In attenuated form, its work even managed to survive the onslaught. It was moving to observe how the many groups defended by Father Gleb rallied behind him in their turn after his arrest. An appeal by three Pentecostalists on behalf of this Orthodox priest was unprecedented, but a welcome event in the life of a man who had already shown himself to be one of the outstanding ecumenical figures of our age.

In August 1979 Father Gleb issued his most radical statement so far, a lengthy examination of the situation of the Russian Orthodox Church and containing such proposals as the deliberate creation of unregistered (illegal) parishes outside state control and the holding of secret ordinations to create a parallel structure to the Moscow Patriarchate. The hope was that this would take the pressure off the latter, averting the state's eyes to the new initiative. In calling for such a policy, he pointed to the success of Soviet Catholics and Protestants in doing something similar.

His arrest followed on 1 November 1979, after which the KGB twice searched his flat, on the second occasion stripping his wife, elder daughter and a friend naked in the process.

On 28 August 1980 a Moscow court sentenced Father Gleb, after a four-day trial, to ten years, half in confinement, half in exile. The charge was brought under the notorious Article 70, which deals with 'anti-Soviet activity', and the episode forms one of the most disgraceful Soviet acts against the Church in post-war years. Western public opinion has barely rallied to his defence, even when in the autumn of 1981 he smuggled a heartbreaking letter out of his prison camp in the Urals, begging people in the West, including me personally, to intervene on his behalf to ask that he should be given a Bible to comfort him in his cell. Not to be able to help him, not to be able to persuade the Church in the West to speak out, leaves one feeling angry and sad.

Positively, however, the example of Father Gleb and a few others like him has done much to restore the moral authority of Russian Orthodoxy for the youngest generation of Soviet people.

2

A Seeking Generation

Anatoli Levitin, a man who has had great influence over young people in the Soviet Union down the years, first as a teacher of literature, then as a publicist and defender of religious liberty, and who is now in exile in Switzerland, writes:

Young people today in the USSR continue to be drawn to religion. Why is this? General disillusionment with Marxism–Leninism is one important factor. The infallibility of Soviet ideology received a fatal blow in 1956 when Stalin was dethroned. Now young people no longer take Marxism–Leninism seriously, so there is an ideological vacuum. How is this vacuum usually filled? Mostly, sad to say, with alcohol. But some young people with intellectual interests turn to politics and embark on the road of open oposition to the regime, forming the main reservoir of the Russian democratic movement. . . . Young intellectuals in the towns find their way to religion through conscious and prolonged searching, whereas workers and peasants in the provinces are drawn to faith because of an elemental impulse, which comes from the subconscious and is inspired. The urban intellectual youth usually join the Orthodox Church, but in the provinces young people usually turn to one of the many different religious sects which exist outside the Orthodox Church.

The Russian Orthodox Church attracts both the most educated and the most backward sections of the population. Those who fall between these two groups have mostly left the Church. Religious faith (at least openly expressed) is rare amongst the middle-aged (30–50). The highest proportion of church-goers are so-called 'old grannies' (*babushki*) – the old women. In the 1920s I used to be told that the old folk were dying off and that the Church would also die. Twenty years then passed and in 1947 a deacon, who was a superficial and ignorant man, said: 'Whatever will happen when the old people die and no one is left in the Church?' But since then another thirty years have passed and not only are there no fewer church-goers, there are more. Still old women predominate. Most of them have had little education; they are cleaning women, domestic workers and women who work in collective farms. Unlike in the 1920s, it cannot now be claimed that religion is a survival of the past, since seventy-five per cent of the old women who go to church today were the *Komsomol* members of the past and went to Soviet Schools. It cannot now be asserted that religion is the prop of the ruling classes of the past, since most of these old women come from worker or peasant backgrounds and can remember nothing of pre-revolutionary ways. After all, those who are in their seventies today were only ten at the time of the Revolution, and so have lived most of their lives under Soviet rule. But apart from the old women, it is the young people aged between eighteen and thirty who are now going to church. As a rule, they are members of the intelligentsia, students, young specialists, sometimes young artists and writers. They start by being disillusioned with the ruling ideology and begin seeking 'the truth'. This milieu of the young Soviet intelligentsia is most receptive to religion. You can sense religious ideas in the air when you are with these youngsters, so that sometimes only the gentlest of nudges is needed to bring someone to faith. Two and a half years ago in Leningrad I remember talking to a young man who became interested in religion after reading an article by Lenin, 'Lev Tolstoy as a mirror of the Russian Revolution', which had been part of his syllabus at school. Lenin described Tolstoy as 'a prince, become a fool in Christ' and this caught his attention. So he determined to read all the religious works of Tolstoy, which was no easy task, since these books cannot be found in most libraries. Then he became interested in the theology of Metropolitan Makari and various other Orthodox theological works. As a result, when I met this young man he had become an Orthodox believer who went to church every day and had applied for a place at a seminary. He is by no means unique. I have met several hundred like him.

Father Dimitri Dudko's discussions in the Church of St Nicholas on Preobrazhenka in Moscow were a unique event. They took place in the first half of 1974, and on the way there you could see at the tram stop a group of youngsters in modern-looking clothes asking how to find the church. When you got there the church would be packed with such a strange crowd that it was hard to believe that this was not a youth club. There was no sign of the 'old women of God'. Here there was almost exclusively the younger generation.

Young people like this formed the group who were the constant companions of Father Dmitri and other popular Moscow priests, and many of them were guests at my home, too. As a rule, they rarely went to church; Church Slavonic was alien to them and their atheist education; and religious rituals confused them. They would start by reading religious literature, and would often meet believers to argue and talk about religion. Gradually, however, they would be overwhelmed by a desire to pray, and would begin turning to prayer more and more as life threw up difficulties in their path. Slowly they would become accustomed to the atmosphere in church; communion would become a spiritual necessity to them.

The conversion of young educated people to the Orthodox Church is a phenomenon of large towns and intellectual circles, but in the provinces it is the sects which are growing. The Soviet government is mortally afraid of sectarianism, because it is difficult to control and impossible to tame. Moreover, the sects in Russia have a huge membership and are deeply rooted in the people. In the 1920s members of sects waged war on the Orthodox Church, tearing from it a sizeable proportion of the people, but now they face the same enemy as the Orthodox – atheism. The sects operate mainly among the broad masses, leaving the intelligentsia practically untouched. The Baptists are the most wide-spread of the sectarian movements. Baptist converts are often young men from the country or from a small town, they are collective-farm or factory workers, metal-smiths, carpenters or unskilled labourers. They might be white-collar workers, draughtsmen, accountants or technicians. They have been deeply offended by the unrelieved vulgarity of Soviet life – by the all-pervading deception, disgusting fawning, cowardice and unrestrained drunkenness among the young, the debauchery, careerism and the totally selfish search for personal gain. Such young converts know no literature or only what they were taught at school; they are not used to reading. An Orthodox church service is incomprehensible to them with its unfamiliar language, rituals, strange clothes and wailing old women. After just a few minutes such a person shrugs his shoulders and leaves. Then he meets a simple person like himself who gives him a book containing these words on the title page: 'The Holy Gospel of Our Lord Jesus Christ'. He starts reading. Much of it is beyond him, much surprises him; but then he begins to read the Sermon on the Mount. Simple, clear words, something concerned with living today. He is soon introduced to Evangelical Christians and meets people as simple as himself, but people who do not drink alcohol, do not smoke, who reject debauchery and foul language. This is so unlike everything that surrounds him that these people seem to him to have come from another planet. . . .

True, on closer acquaintance the Baptist way will not by any means satisfy everyone. The man who has a need for the mystical will not be satisfied. A meeting of Baptists always reminds me of a house-management committee meeting: first comes the sermon, sometimes deep, original,

27

talented, but more often rather stereotyped; then several hymns and a discussion on current concerns. There is no depth, mystery, nothing reaching beyond the bounds of this world, no ardent prayer. Therefore many who come to the Baptists do not stay. They are looking for a more deeply mystical experience, for richer religious food. For this reason, mystical sects such as the Pentecostals, Seventh-Day Adventists and Jehovah's Witnesses are growing, despite cruel persecution. These ecstatic sects are gaining most of their converts from amongst young workers and peasants.

All this indicates that Russian youth, awakening from its long sleep, is searching, that it has set out upon a journey. As a child I loved to walk to the early liturgy in the winter. The Petersburg winter was cold and dark. Life had not yet awoken. The occasional person in the street would be hurrying to work; he would slip, get up and start off again. And there, in the distance, would be the church which had only just been opened. It would still be empty; only the odd pilgrim would be there, placing candles before the icons. One could feel the silence and expectation everywhere. I often feel that Russia is experiencing such a time of expectation now. The night is over. The sleepers are waking up. Life is beginning to stir. What will the day be like? (*Religion in Communist Lands*, No. 4, 1979, pp. 234–7).

Levitin has put his finger on perhaps the single most important factor in religious life in the Soviet Union today: the emergence of a younger generation of seekers, seekers who sometimes find. This guarantees not only the survival of the faith into the twenty-first century, but is also something of major importance in the whole development of world Christianity. The servility of the Moscow Patriarchate in its unconditional support of Soviet policy might have been expected to deter, but with perspicacity the younger generation is coming to see that this is not something which is of the essence of Orthodoxy and the total integrity of Father Gleb and others gives a moral leadership which replaces the vacuum which would otherwise have existed.

Even when I was a student at Moscow University over twenty years ago (1959–60) I met young people in this highly-selective training ground for the country's future leadership who were seeking something. They were still coming to terms with the shock of Khrushchev's denunciation of Stalin three years previously. In their search to find something to replace the fallen idol, I did not feel, I most honestly confess, that it would be religion which would supply the answer, but now I am rather inclined to think that was an over-hasty judgement.

I do not propose in this chapter to say anything about the revival among young people in the Protestant and Roman Catholic Churches, having done so at length about each respectively in *Faith on Trial in Russia* (1971) and *Land of Crosses* (1979). Suffice it to say that Anatoli Levitin's remarks above have substance. The Catholic Church seems to be gaining in influence daily among the young in Lithuania, where it is the traditional faith, though much less is known about Catholicism in other areas where it is more marginally present. The Baptist Church, by the evangelical presentation of the basic message, by fervent prayer (I disagree with Levitin above when he denies this element in the Baptist faith) and by its concern for the well-being of its members, has had a considerable impact upon the young in many parts of the Soviet Union.

The discovery of the Orthodox Church by the young is less dramatic, though in the light of the traditional identification of the Russian people with it over the centuries this may well prove to be a phenomenon of greater permanence and more lasting significance.

Nothing in this revival of Orthodoxy is quantifiable. Some western visitors go to churches, see a preponderance of old people, just as there used to be twenty or even sixty years ago, and they conclude that this talk of a revival is wishful thinking. Yet its existence is a fact which can be proved. To do this one need go no further than to recount the violent reaction to the existence of a 'Christian seminar',[1] a seemingly-innocuous discussion group which the KGB has used every means at its disposal to crush, and several of whose members are now undergoing periods of imprisonment or forced internment in psychiatric hospitals.

Those newly converted to Orthodoxy were of course attracted to the ritual and devotion of the liturgy, but they also needed a forum where they could discuss the philosophical implications of their young faith and its practical effect on the *mores* of their everyday lives and relationships. In the words of Alexander Ogorodnikov, who founded the Christian seminar in Moscow in 1974:

> As we were dissatisfied with the mere 'performance of a religious cult', had had no opportunity to receive a religious education and needed to establish brotherly Christian relations, we began in October 1974 to hold a religious and philosophical seminar. . . . Our thirst for spiritual communion, religious education and missionary service runs up against all the might of the state's repressive machinery.

Discussions ranged between subjects as widely contrasted as the nineteenth-century Russian philosopher and mystic, Vladimir Solovyov, and Billy Graham. They not only felt the need to meet and talk, but they also invited more mature Christians to talk to them and they founded a periodical called *Obshchina* (Community) in *samizdat* (unofficial publication), an initiative suppressed by the KGB almost as soon as it had begun. The seminar seems to have adopted no formal statement of aims, it has no structure and no finances. Of necessity, many of its activities have had to be secret, therefore we have no comprehensive idea of the extent of its influence, which one suspects still to be small and confined to one or two major cities. It would not be surprising to find,

[1] I am indebted to an article by Jane Ellis in *Religion in Communist Lands*, vol. 8, No. 2 (Summer 1980), pp. 92–105, for the information in this chapter from this point on.

however, that other similar but unconnected groups exist elsewhere.

Alexander Ogorodnikov was no more than twenty-eight when he was arrested in November 1978. He had gone through the academic and professional training necessary for a career in films. At the Cinematographical Institute in Moscow his interest in Christianity was first aroused when he saw a private showing of Pasolini's film, *The Gospel According to St Matthew*. Ogorodnikov described the spiritual quest of his friends and himself in these words:

My friends and I grew up in atheist families. Each of us has come along a complicated, sometimes agonizing path of spiritual searching. From Marxist convictions, through nihilism and through the total rejection of any ideology at all, through an attraction to the 'hippy' lifestyle, we have come to the Church.

This open rejection of the official state ideology, particularly on the part of gifted young intellectuals, must form the basic reason for the persecution of the group, for their activities were deliberately quiet and did not stray much into the area of religious liberty and human rights. After an initial one-year sentence for 'parasitism', Ogorodnikov was not released and his second trial took place in Kalinin in 1980. On 8 September he was sentenced to six years' strict regime camp, to be followed by five years' exile under Article 70 of the Penal Code.

The only founding member of the group considerably older than the rest, Tatyana Shchipkova, was fifty when she was arrested and sentenced in January 1980 to three years in a labour camp. Like other members of the seminar, she was not accused of activities directly connected with it, but was charged with 'malicious hooliganism'. Her sentence was a travesty of justice. What malicious hooliganism there had been was on the part of the militia, one of whom physically assaulted her in attempting to confiscate a notebook from her during a raid on the Moscow flat where a meeting of the

Christian seminar was taking place. She apparently slapped
his face in pain and self-defence.

To represent the thinking and activity of this new generation of Orthodox I have chosen Vladimir Poresh. He was
born in 1949 and came under the influence of Tatyana
Shchipkova at the age of seventeen. Her account of her spor-
adic contacts with him over his formative years is perhaps the
most persuasive description of a recent conversion to the
Orthodox Church which has reached us and it is worth quot-
ing at length:

In the autumn of 1966 my first-year French class was joined
by Volodya Poresh, who was then seventeen years old – a
tall adolescent with large hands and honest, kind eyes, a
simple person without the faintest suspicion of the existence
of the camps and convinced that religion developed as the
result of fear of the forces of nature. He soon began to work
in my group. After each lecture he would ask me questions,
delighting me with the lack of banality of his vision and
the accuracy of his argument. It was a pity to lose such a
pupil, but I was glad when he was able to go on to Leningrad University.

He was very much alone in Leningrad. Thrown back on
his own reflections, he at last came face to face with questions of universal significance. His anxiety found expression
in his letters of that period. First of all he realized the
senselessness of life without spirituality:

'All too often recently I have been faced with questions
that have no answer, like a machine in perpetual motion.
It is as if I have gone into a room where I have seen a
mechanism – no one knows how it works or the reason
it is there, or even why it was made. First of all, I saw
that the world was senseless, like a cat running across
the street. Everything is senseless from beginning to
end. . . . Then it suddenly seemed that the most senseless
things had more sense than anything else. Art, literature,
science, all sorts of interests, hobbies, quite useless things

– all this seemed more important than the rest. All spiritual life is senseless because it brings people nothing but suffering. But all the same it is the most important thing. . . . It is senseless to keep searching, but I shall go on searching for this very reason' (24 December 1969).

And at last, after these meanderings, the crisis came in 1970: the total recognition of his own spiritual enslavement and that of everyone around him. He came to Smolensk for the winter holidays. He seemed so completely changed that I thought there had been some sort of catastrophe and fearfully asked him what had happened. He sat down without taking off his coat and said: 'I understand everything!' 'What do you mean, everything?' 'Everything!' I understood of course because I, too, could not think of anything else at that time and had reached the same dead end. We were both heading towards the same conclusion in different ways, with an age difference of nineteen years. These were not the sort of questions that each generation meets when its time comes, but those that time offers all its contemporaries, irrespective of their age when these questions overtake them. 'I cannot live when people spit in my face every day.' He admitted then that at that time he was close to suicide. He found the way out later: 'I came to the conclusion that God exists. He cannot not exist, otherwise there would be no sense in anything.' But faith was still a long way from this deduction. To become involved in life, to discover its meaning and become its embodiment – this was what he was striving for. I forget which month it was in 1973 when he arrived in a joyful and enthusiastic mood and told me: 'I have begun a new phase in my life. I've got to know someone called Sasha Ogorodnikov. We have decided to create a culture within a culture.' His search for a spiritual foundation for this culture led him to Russian religious philosophy: 'Besides this, I'm reading Russian philosophy now.' He went on:

'I'm discovering a number of very interesting things. I've read Berdyaev's essay on Khomyakov, a few things by

33

Solovyov and some Dostoevsky. And it seems that the climax of twentieth-century western philosophy, existentialism, can also be seen in a more or less developed form in Khomyakov: that is, not a philosophy of abstract concepts, but a philosophy of life. There's still a lot that I don't yet understand. I find it all fairly difficult. But yet it's very important to me. . . . I shall write to you in more detail when I have sorted it all out' (February 1974).

Volodya was baptized on 20 October 1974. The slow, difficult process of involvement in the Church had begun. He was helped in this by his good qualities: intellectual versatility, the inability to stagnate, his constant striving towards a critical re-evaluation of what has already been established.

There follows a description of Poresh's reflection on the importance of joining the Orthodox Church.

Thus the idea of the church community was born: Volodya is with us, with the seminar and with the community. He is linked to all of us by an indestructible thread which no detention or imprisonment can break. It is an indissoluble mystical bond. This is what he wrote this year to my son Alexander Shchipkov, who was serving in the army:
    'Sanya, don't forget to pray at 10 o'clock in the morning or later. This has very great mystical significance. . . . Despite the heavy blows we have borne, we are all strong as never before. You would be very glad if you could see us. Prayers are a great help to those going through an ordeal. We pray for all of you when we gather together. Sanya, keep your spirits up! The inner conflict continues, we are sent these trials for our enlightenment and transformation' (*Religion in Communist Lands*, No. 2, 1980, pp. 101–2).

So, having been baptized at the age of 25, Vladimir Poresh became a founding member of Ogorodnikov's Christian seminar and worked on *Obshchina*. He immediately came under police surveillance, even open hounding in the streets through which he walked to see friends. He recounts the treatment he received in an article which he wrote for the one issue of *Obshchina* (No. 2) which did reach the West before it was suppressed. In the same article he gives a description of the atmosphere in the Christian seminar in Moscow, which he attended on his frequent visits from Leningrad:

> At 25 Prospekt Mira, Sasha (Ogorodnikov) was employed as a janitor in a tuberculosis clinic and had been given a shed to live in – a tiny building with two rooms, a hall and a kitchen with a gas stove, a small table and a sink. It was not designed for habitation: once it had been a carpenter's workshop. It was difficult to heat in winter, and there was only a small barred window to let in the light. But of course there are worse places than that one – all the more so because we loved that little flat for the spirit of freedom which filled it. It was there that we held our seminars on religion and philosophy; in other words, where we discussed the questions which were most important for us: questions of religion and life. The door of that house was open to all and anyone could take part and speak. Newcomers were struck by the variety there: they might meet old men or sixteen-year-old hippies, scholars or speculators. Those conversations, that way of life, took hold of me completely: it was all so sound, so full of meaning and depth, so full of the warmth and genuine feeling which you cannot confuse with anything else; it was so different from vulgar Soviet life that I always hurried to Moscow, to Sasha, to that flat, with my whole being. It had become palpably obvious to us that it was very easy to live according to the truth. You just had to make a determined stand against the pressures of the frantic world and God would help you and strengthen your convictions (*Religion in Communist Lands*, No. 2, 1980, p. 103).

Vladimir Poresh was arrested on 1 August 1979 and later

sentenced to five years' strict regime camps, followed by three years' internal exile. News coming from Perm Prison Camp No. 35 reported him to be in bad health, but with enough resistance still to declare a hunger strike in protest against the confiscation of his Bible.

In 1980, a Russian Orthodox believer who had been very active in the struggle for religious liberty in the USSR had an unexpected visitor. Late one evening, he answered a knock on his door to find a young man of about twenty-four on the doorstep. The young men was well dressed and had an 'affluent' (by Soviet standards) look about him.

Without any preliminaries, the young man asked if he had come to the house of so and so. Having established that this was indeed that person, the young man said: 'I'm facing a terrible dilemma. You must help me. I know your name and I think you may be able to help me resolve my problem. I've suddenly begun to believe in God and I simply don't know what to do about it. It's terrible!'

His host had considerable trouble keeping a straight face but managed to, because the young man was quite obviously and sincerely distressed. It emerged that the young man came from a very well placed 'Party' family, had been brought up to be an atheist and to accept the directives of the Party as indisputable truths.

Studying at Moscow University, he had to do a special project and decided, being an 'active' atheist, to make a study of the pernicious religious broadcasts beamed at the Soviet Union from the West. The result was totally unexpected.

'Two Sundays ago', recounted the young man, 'I was listening to the Russian religious broadcast of the BBC when suddenly, in the middle of the programme, for no reason at all I realized that I had come to believe in God. Just like that. One minute I didn't believe and the next minute I did. I was horrified, tried to reason myself out of it, thinking I was suffering from some momentary aberration. But it just didn't work. No matter what I said to myself to try to counter this sudden belief, it had absolutely no effect. Since then I have

36

been quite desperate: I feel as if the ground has been whipped away from under my feet. I don't know what to think or what to do. The only thing I know with any certainty is that I believe in God.'

The young man had tried to talk to his parents about the problem, but they were first amused, then incredulous and finally aghast.

'I had heard your name mentioned on western radio', concluded the young man, 'and I know that you are a believer. So I managed to find out your address and my only hope now is that you can help me somehow find myself, or direct me to someone else who could do so.'

Fortunately his host, who had become an active believer as an adult, was able to understand and sympathize with the predicament in which the young man found himself. As well as giving advice from his own experience, he undertook to acquaint the young man with other believers in student circles and to introduce him to church-going and Bible study.

For each such story that one hears, there must be hundreds, throughout the vastness of the Soviet Union, that never reach the outside world.

PART II

Spiritual Experience
of Russian Orthodoxy

3

The Challenge

I was standing in the church in total darkness. Although I
was protected in a little enclosure at the front I knew the
church must be full, not only because we had had to shoulder
our way through twelve thousand people shut outside by
calling out '*inostrantsy*' (foreigners), not because any murmur
of a multitude broke the silence, but because I could feel the
tension, the spiritual expectancy if you like, which the faithful
generated.

Sometimes at Orthodox Easter there was trouble. This
often affected first the procession going around the outside of
the church at the very beginning of the service, symbolically
looking for the body of Christ. As Alexander Solzhenitsyn
recounts in one of his finest pages, this procession had to
contend not only with a vast gathering of people, but often
also with the active hostility of hooligans encouraged by the
police. This year there was calm. The sound of a distant,
mournful chant. It grew louder as the deacons and priests
approached the main door: 'They have taken away my Lord
and I know not where they have laid him.' A hammering and
creaking from the back indicated a great door opening.
'Whom seek ye?' 'The body of Jesus.' 'Why seek ye the living
among the dead? He is not here. He is risen – *Khristos voskrese!*'.
For the first time the great crowd broke its silence. A murmur,
as though they could not believe the truth they were affirming:
Voistinu voskrese ('Is risen indeed') was their antiphon. But
now too there was light. Someone at the back had lit the first
paschal candle, a single point of light not able to penetrate
the darkness. But then there was another, and another.
Swiftly the flame passed from hand to hand. I began to see

what I had not known. Every one of the worshippers held a candle. In less than a minute the church was a blaze of light – no, not the impersonal glare of electricity – it was five thousand individual flames united in one faith. Each candle lit up a face behind it. That face bore the deep lines of sorrow, of personal tragedy. Yet, as it was illuminated, the suffering turned to joy, to the certain knowledge of the reality of the risen Lord. Seeing my empty hands, an old lady reached out to me across the low rail. I could hardly hear her say, '*Khristos voskrese*', above the exultant shouts that now came from the worshippers, but as I replied I felt the barriers of nationality and culture fall away. I was one of them.

Often since that Easter midnight when I was a student in Moscow twenty-two years ago have I reflected how that single five minutes of experience taught me the certainty of the resurrection in a way that reading a hundred theological books during my undergraduate days had not quite managed to do. 'How could they be so sure?' I asked myself. The answer always came back: they have trodden the way of the cross to the hill of Calvary. Their suffering under Stalin stripped them of every material advantage and reward; they were imprisoned; dear ones died in every family. Today's policies consistently make the ordinary Christian a second-class citizen. Even now prison is the destiny of the fearless evangelist. They do not debate the resurrection: they have experienced its reality in their own lives. They have not pre-served the faith in hostile surroundings; it has preserved them. Their joy is truly a glimpse through the curtain which divides us from heaven.

Many times since, I had felt a wound in my own heart when I have heard Evangelical Christians say – especially in America – 'Orthodoxy? It's nearly all superstition. I pray that the Russians will become born-again Christians. They need to know Jesus as their personal saviour.' Words have no meaning to me if the resurrection experience of the Russian Orthodox believer is not a new birth, if it was not the certainty of personal salvation which transformed suffering into joy on those faces before me as I watched them. I was overwhelmed spiritually by my first experience of the living Christ in the Soviet Union.

On another occasion an old lady approached me in an Orthodox church, noticed the filth of Russian autumn mud on my boots and insisted on washing it off with her own hands underneath the primitive jet of a hand-pumped water supply at the corner of the street by the church. If she could thus affect me, who had had considerable experience of the church from my earliest days, by acting out the gospel story of Christ's washing the disciples feet, it is hardly surprising that atheists from the West have actually been brought to the faith by their exposure to the living Christ in the Soviet Union. I think of another British exchange student, Antony Hippisley, converted by his meeting with Russian Christians in 1964, who went on to celebrate his marriage to an American girl in the Moscow Baptist church. Then a decade later there was another British exchange student with no interest in religion who was persuaded by a Russian friend to listen to Father Dmitri Dudko's question-and-answer sermons in an Orthodox church. Father Dmitri's church had become a centre of attraction for young Muscovites in the early seventies. The student listened to the examples Father Dmitri gave, illustrating the faith of children, and later wrote:

What did it all mean? Well to me, then an atheist, just this. The immorality of Soviet society, its inhumanity and corruption, its lack of a moral code or credible ideals, means that Christ's teaching comes through to those whom it reaches as a shining contrast. It stresses the value of the individual, of humaneness, forgiveness, gentleness, love. It was this that appealed to the child in his example. As for me, the atheist, Father Dmitri that evening convinced me that the moral code of Christianity was not just something that could be cast aside as superseded; that, in fact, it had survived for two thousand years precisely because it did stress certain qualities essential in personal relations be-

43

tween men. The loss of these qualities is one of the most disturbing features of modern Soviet life. [After the service Father Dmitri was taken away by two unknown men.] And so he disappeared: the bravest man and one of the best I have ever seen. I shall never forget him (*Religion in Communist Lands*, No. 2, 1976, pp. 23, 27).

If the Russian Church could thus impress itself on the consciousness of someone who had been brought up to experience the richness and variety of life in the West, is it not likely the more to affect young Russians whose whole psychology and upbringing have been moulded by conformism to the status quo, by atheism, by the sheer hypocrisy of the ceaseless barrage of propaganda? For those who have not experienced this, it is difficult to illustrate just how grey and monotonous is Soviet life in the countryside, how ferociously any sort of independent intellectual enquiry is discouraged, how even any exploration of the true application of Marx's thought to the conditions of the present day is barred to those who wish to make a career within the present system.

The sermons of Father Dmitri therefore broke right into the lives of young people in Moscow. To hear the gospel presented in terms of living reality, treating their day-to-day problems in concrete Christian terms, not only brought people young and old flocking into the church of St Nicholas, but held their attention and presented a challenge which had never been found in the newspapers, or on radio and television.

In the truest sense of the word, Father Dmitri was presenting an evangelical message, one from which Evangelicals in the West can learn. One can read his words and appreciate his wrestling with the problems of presenting the gospel to an atheist society in his book, *Our Hope*.

As Father Vsevolod Shpiller, another outstanding preacher of the Orthodox Church in Moscow, said to his congregation in a Lenten sermon in 1969:

I believe that a new chapter is beginning in the history of

44

our church. Our Orthodox faith, by concerted efforts from various sides, had already long ago reached the 'under-privileged', as they said in the last century. Today it has clearly ceased to be the property simply of the illiterate, pious granny, preserved by and relying on a superstitious and purely external form of the faith. The request from my parishioners [to give these talks] testifies to this. . . . More and more frequently and unexpectedly you meet people of the most varied ages and situations who have gone through deep inner spiritual, mental and emotional crises, some-times through tragic conflicts which they have found in-soluble in a non-religious framework. Not infrequently now, here and there, maybe in a muted and novel way, some-times questioningly, the poet's words can be heard: 'Not long ago I was secretly told Christ would soon return' (*Religion in Communist Lands*, No. 3, 1973, p. 23).

This awakening has given birth to a new Christian litera-ture in the Soviet Union. It is hard to judge how much there is and how widely it spreads, as none of it can be published there, but one suspects that there is considerably more of it than we know about for certain. The clandestine Christian writings of the 1930s which helped to preserve the faith in such difficult times are still surfacing. We know enough about the recent literature to see it as clear evidence of the growing faith to which Father Vsevolod referred above. A definite tendency in some circles is to seek to make relevant for today the 'Slavophilism' of the nineteenth century, the belief that Orthodoxy and Russia are inseparable and that the soul of Russia is more 'Christian' than that of other countries.

There is a certain danger here, which should not be over-looked alongside the very real attraction of this viewpoint. One's basic unease is over the long-term future, rather than the present, if such a philosophy becomes dominant. Such a force may well be explosive enough to shift the dead weight of the present status quo, but it could also unlock deep-seated feelings which might boil over uncontrollably. However, these are problems created by the Soviets themselves and on their present course it is impossible to see how the leaders can avoid the eventual release of waves of resentment against former oppressors. In a multi-racial society, such as the Soviet Union is, the domination of one race, the Russians, is bound eventually to cause a backlash when this is broken. In the Baltic States or Soviet Central Asia, the Slav is inevitably seen as a colonialist oppressor, though Solzhenitsyn's argument that the Russian, too, is deeply oppressed by the system is also correct.

Here is an anonymous example of the new Russian nationalism from the now-suppressed *samizdat* journal *Veche*, the former editor of which, Vladimir Osipov, was arrested in 1974 and condemned to an eight-year sentence. The words express a hopeful note, even while surveying a scene of desolation:

> They say it is winter now. 'Winter wants to be.' But I think that spring is on the way. Torrents of spring. Floods. An inundation, if you like. Winter being over, spring thoughts have awakened in everyone. A torrent of thoughts. They are difficult to hold back . . . Orthodoxy and Russia, Russia and Orthodoxy. You think this funny? Listen, why do you think it funny? Perhaps 'atheism and Russia' sounds better? Russia and atheism? Don't you find that funny? Do you remember such a cry? At the most critical moments it was these words which used to ring out: 'For the faith, the Tsar and the fatherland'. You think this even funnier? What a breath of the past, of the archaic! . . . But this was the most sacred, the most self-sacrificing of cries. They died with it on their lips and hoped to enter the Kingdom of God. . . . There is no Tsar now. The fatherland remains. Or perhaps it does not?
>
> On no battlefield has anyone yet cried, 'For atheism'. And the Russian air has not been sanctified by such a cry. Atheism is something alien, imported, not part of us. I think that atheism was imposed on Russia and has not

taken root in it. In the Russian land, as the philosophers affirm, atheism becomes a faith. Atheism is the dark side of faith. Do you remember the first years of the Revolution? With what religious fervour they destroyed everything! They destroyed – and now we sit on the ruins. We sit and think about what we have done. We sit and grieve over the ruins of our churches, of our history. . . . People have begun to awaken. A surprising thing is happening: the sons of Communists are becoming Christians. . . .

Russia is saved by Orthodoxy. Orthodoxy is indestructible. It is God's work and a Russian can be only Orthodox (*Religion in Communist Lands*, No. 1, 1973, pp. 21–5).

Alexander Ogorodnikov and Boris Razveyev, writing as young men a few years after the above essay, analyse the reasons why the new generation cares enough about the Orthodox faith which it is finding to sacrifice for it not only education and prospects, but even, if necessary, its liberty. They wish to embrace the Orthodox faith and the dynamic understanding of life it gives them, after being brought up in the ossified cage of the official ideology. This is an extract from a letter they wrote to Dr Philip Potter, General Secretary of the World of Council of Churches, in July 1976:

Russian culture today, while pushing its way out from under the rubble of terror, lies and delusions, has given birth to an intellectual ferment which neither we ourselves nor the world in general expected. As it emerged from the chaos of underground life, misunderstood and undervalued by the world and sometimes regarded with hostility, it was at first just a cry of pain, a desperate attempt to escape from the thrill of spiritual captivity by ideology. After tearing the mask off the state myth, this movement made itself known to the world, asserting only its zealous rejection of that myth and its single-minded thirst for freedom. As part of our critical approach, we proceeded to overthrow all idols, to suspect all ideologies in principle, and we ended up in the ontological void of this world. This world, once

47

so near and dear to us, suddenly lost its dimensions, the explored contours of its height and depth, and was deprived of meaning and perspective.

We found ourselves in a new blind alley. Having begun our rebellion in the name of human freedom, we eliminated the human element. . . . Taking man as the measure of all things, we thereby deprived him of any standard by which to measure himself. Modern non-religious humanism, in declaring man to be the highest and only standard of value, ends up by justifying all his actions, even the evil he has done in history. And we have experienced for ourselves the wholly relative nature of humanist morality, transformed into a terrible attempt to devalue the human personality, which without God becomes merely a 'social animal' or a pattern 'moulded' by the social system.

It was at this point that a revision of our moral values became necessary, and we began to strive openly for self-realization within the flow of history and thought. Expelled from academic circles by the will of history, driven off the pages of books by censorship, and into a night-watchman's cubicle, aspiring Russian thought matured in agonizing disputes (sometimes lasting for weeks), which opened up to us the truth of Russian religious philosophy. Fathers Sergei Bulgakov and Georges Florovsky brought us to the threshold of the church and set us before its doors.

And our ailing souls heard at last the quiet call of *God*. The world was transformed, it acquired wholeness and integrity (*Religion in Communist Lands*, No. 1, 1979, p. 49).

Such wrestling with the eternal truths of man and God illustrates a very positive hope within the neo-Slavophile tendency, which makes one regret the more the suppression of the debate on such issues in the Soviet Union today. The new generation of Orthodox Christians is calling upon the Church to be less passive than hitherto in its efforts to transmit the faith. Yevgeni Barabanov, a specialist in fine art who has written several challenging essays on the relevance of the old faith to modern life, has called for a Christian initiative to counter the 'godless humanism' which is destroying mankind (*From Under the Rubble*, p. 192, a collection of essays edited by Solzhenitsyn and published in English in 1975). Barabanov says that the Church itself must generate this missionary zeal and explain the nature of the hope which Christianity offers to the world.

There are already signs that this is happening in a few places. While by far the best-known example is Father Dmitri Dudko's question-and-answer sermons, this is not an isolated one, even though the state has shown itself determined to crack down on this kind of activity since 1979. Many more now, both clergy and laity, are dedicated to proclaiming the evangelical witness of the Orthodox Church. An eye-witness in *Religion in Communist Lands* (No. 4–5, 1974, pp. 8–11) described the 'jours fixes' (open house held on a certain day of the week) which took place in the 1960s at Semkhoz, near Zagorsk in the Moscow region, at the home of Father Alexander Men.

The 'jour fixe' would begin in total informality. Leaving Moscow's Yaroslavsky Station at 3.15 in the afternoon, the young people would begin their discussions on the train itself during the two hours of the journey. Conversation would continue avidly all afternoon and often not finish until the group had arrived back in Moscow late that night. Father Alexander would come into the garden to meet his guests, he would bless them and in the summer they would spend the whole evening on the verandah discussing any question which came up on literature, art, politics and the Christian faith. His library was open to all, a collection of philosophy and religious literature such as could not be found in a single public library anywhere in the country. Despite the rarity of his books, he would lend them freely and sometimes they would pass from hand to hand for a year before they came back. After the Soviet invasion of Czechoslovakia in 1968 Father Alexander closed down these seminars because he did not like the sharp political tone which the discussions were acquiring, but of course they continue in other forms elsewhere.

Some priests demonstrate their responsibility to the young by producing *samizdat* manuscripts which interpret the liturgy for ,the convert and the Foyer Oriental Chrétien in Brussels has done good work in publishing some of these in Russian.

On my first visit to Siberia in 1979 I met a young parish priest in Irkutsk who welcomed the whole party of British tourists with whom I was travelling. Very unusually, the Intourist guide sent for the priest to meet our group and encouraged discussion. One of the group asked him what he had been doing before he moved to this church. He replied, 'I was working as a missionary.' He had been assigned to the Orthodox Church in Ulan-Ude, the capital of the Buryat Mongol Autonomous Republic, where the bulk of the population is Buddhist. One cannot really imagine that such a remark could have been made until recently, though we should never forget that the Orthodox Church did originally evangelize Siberia during the drive of the Russian Empire eastwards from the fifteenth to the nineteenth centuries. This illustrates that the Orthodox Church is not just passively awaiting the return of the young, but is actively going out to seek converts, even though, as far as is known, this is on the initiative of individuals, rather than a response to an overall strategy, which almost certainly does not exist.

4

Prayer

Although my experience of prayer in the Soviet Union is not
that extensive, I have participated in and read enough about
it to realize that here is another area of the Christian life
where we have much to learn from these underprivileged
people. A generation of western Christians, from Evangelicals
to Catholics, have enriched their prayer lives by listening to
the broadcasts and reading the books on prayer of Archbishop
Antony Bloom, for many years incumbent of the Russian
Orthodox Church (Moscow jurisdiction) in London. These
in themselves are an antidote to those whose casual acquaintance with the Russian Church leads them to believe that such
prayer as the Orthodox enjoy is collective, formalistic and
virtually meaningless. This is the exact opposite of the truth.
The deprivation, both economic and spiritual (in the sense,
for example, of being virtually cut off from Christian literature), which has on the surface depressed Russian Christianity for nearly three-quarters of a century, has had the
converse effect of intensifying all aspects of the Christian
experience. In this there is little distinction to be drawn between Orthodox and Evangelicals, and in this chapter I draw
on my experience of both.

The last Russian prayer meeting I attended was in Siberia,
place of exile, suffering and future economic expansion. I had
come to the one Baptist church in the city of Irkutsk unan-
nounced, but was immediately engulfed by the warmth of the
fellowship. After the two-hour service, so direct in its appeal
to the uncommitted, they motioned me into the pastor's private room. Here, to my surprise, there began another service,
not this time with the accoutrements of music and preaching.

51

It was a simple gathering of the committed – the committed youth. There were about thirty people present, of whom, apart from the pastor, I was by far the oldest. I am not sure how much of what followed was according to a pre-arranged plan, but the whole period was an hour long, almost precisely divided into twelve periods of five minutes each. The group remained on their knees throughout this time with no mat or kneeler to ease the weight of their bodies on the wooden floor. Each of the speakers selected a Bible reading (there were several copies of the Scriptures in the room, despite the severe shortage of the Bible throughout the Soviet Union), followed this by a brief meditation on his or her chosen passage, and concluded with a prayer, an act of praise, confession or intercession, just as the reading suggested. There was no overt thematic connection between what was said by one leader and the next, but the whole amounted to a spectrum of religious experience, the whole life of the suffering Church being urgently revealed before the Creator. If there had been no other Christians in the huge expanse of the Soviet Union, one would have forecast that this cell of prayer alone would have divided, multiplied and worked itself as a leaven into the broad range of communist society, infusing it with the eternal value of the Holy Spirit.

There is a little typewritten book of prayers from the Soviet Union, which reached the Keston College archive in 1974, which shows just how deep is the humility, the readiness to wait upon God, of the Russian Christian. It is lovingly bound and illustrated with pictures of the saints. Here is just a single example of its varied contents, entitled, 'Prayer to Christ for Every Day':

> Lord, grant me to meet with tranquillity of soul all that may befall me this day. Grant that I may obey thy holy will every hour of this day; guide me and maintain me in all things, reveal to me thy will for me and those about me. Whatever news I may receive this day, grant that I may accept it with a tranquil soul and in the firm conviction of

thy holy will in all things. In all my words and deeds, guide my thoughts and emotions, in all unforeseen circumstances let me not forget that all these things are permitted by thee.

Teach me. O Lord, to deal openly and wisely with all, in the community, in my own family . . . , causing grief or embarrassment to no one, but comforting, aiding and counselling all.

Lord, grant me the strength to bear the weariness of the coming day, and all the events that occur in the course of the day.

Guide my will and teach me, O Lord, to pray to thee, to believe, hope, endure patiently, forgive and love (*Religion in Communist Lands*, vol. 3, No. 6, 1975, p. 31).

This theme of self-abasement is not something new in Russian Christianity – indeed it goes right back into history as an ideal. The medieval saints, Boris and Gleb, after whom so many Russian churches are named, are not particularly remarkable in their own right. They were taken up as exemplary figures simply because they were murdered. In the meek acceptance with which they greeted their death, they provided, in the popular view, an ideal which stood out as a guide to future generations.

That same *kenosis*, the abnegation of all human values, the 'emptying himself' which St Paul observed in the person of Christ (Philippians 2: 5–8) is visible in Russian Christianity today. Perhaps the most remarkable literary example of this yet to reach us is contained in a 'Meditation' written by an anonymous young Orthodox Christian in Moscow in 1972 and so far published only in *Religion in Communist Lands* (No. 3, 1976, pp. 43–4). The following is an extract:

My creator, I am your slave, ready for anything, a slave for the humblest task. Yes, a slave – I am not ashamed of that word in our humanist age.

They are ashamed, they do not want to be slaves. They are willing to be scoundrels, but not slaves. They study you. They say that you are not good – and that means that you do not exist. . . .

They, they, they. . . . But I? I, Lord, understand everything and do nothing. Whoever does know and still does what deserves punishment will be beaten all the more. Stopping my foul mouth, full of swearing and spite, I, a 'slave for the humblest task', make no reply to those who insult me, but under my breath I hiss spiteful, nasty oaths. Secretly, on the sly, imperceptibly. For them but not for you. I see that spite is destroying me. For evil designs crawl out of me, like worms out of a corpse, twisting and strangling. Even in the half-hour between confession and Holy Communion I manage to spray out tons of filth from my sick mind and heart. It flies away, only to fall again upon my soul, my pure, snow-white soul, and you, O Lord, do not enter into communion with me.

Again and again and again I repeat with hope, which is stronger than truth: 'O God, be merciful unto me, a sinner!'

And I know. I know as one knows even before one is born, that if I say a quadrillion times, 'O God, be merciful unto me, a sinner!' your strength will flow into me, and the withered, accursed fig tree will revive, flourish, and put forth good, maternal leaves. O my soul, arise! Why are you sleeping?

It will arise, because the grace of God is stronger than earth, than nature, than lameness, than deformity, than spite, than anything which is invincible on earth and it makes doctors shrug their shoulders. . . .

I would love you, Lord, even if you were evil, like a hot, dry wind. I would simply not notice your evilness, just as a normal son loves his father. . . .

I will not hurry you. You yourself know when – when I will be able to drain the cup. Your devoted slave. What a beautiful word!

But prayer in the Russian Church is not just self-abasement. It can also be very strong. Some stir was caused in the late 1960s in the West by the publication of a prayer composed by Alexander Solzhenitsyn, who had up to then been widely, though wrongly, regarded as a secular figure. Ever since, as a marker in my diary, I have carried a picture of Mary and the Infant Jesus, backed by the prayer, containing the words:

> You grant me the clear confidence that You exist, and that You will ensure that not all the ways of goodness are blocked.

No one who has read Solzhenitsyn's *August 1914* will forget, amid the battles and the carnage of the early stages of the war, the scene in which General Samsonov, the night before the decisive battle, seeks solitude in order to pray:

> Just as a jar of sunflower-seed oil, shaken until it is cloudy, needs to stand a while for the dregs to settle to the bottom and for the rest to regain its sunny, transparent colour with a few bubbles floating on the top, so Samsonov longed for some peace and quiet to clarify his mind. He knew what was needed to achieve this: he must pray.
>
> His daily morning and evening prayers, over-familiar and mumbled in haste while his thoughts raced ahead to cope with more mundane matters, were like washing one's hands fully dressed: a mite of cleanliness so small as to be almost imperceptible. But concentrated, dedicated prayer, prayer that was like a hunger that must be satisfied and for which there was no substitute – that kind of prayer, Samsonov recalled, always transformed and fortified him.
>
> Without calling for his orderly Kupchik, he got up, fumbled for matches, lit the little wick of his cut-glass bedside lamp and shot the bolt on the door. He did not draw the curtains, as he was not overlooked from the house opposite.
>
> He opened the little white metal, portable, folding icon and arranged its three panels so that it stood firmly on the table. He lowered himself heavily to his knees without bothering to see whether the floor was clean. Feeling sat-

55

isfaction from the pain in his knees caused by the weight of his ponderous body, he stared at the crucifixion in the central panel of the icon and at the two saints on the smaller side-panels – Saint George and Saint Nicholas. He began to pray.

At first he recited in full two or three familiar prayers: 'Let God arise!', 'Whose dwelleth under the defence of the Most High'; but after that he prayed in a flow of thought that formed itself unconsciously and without spoken words, only occasionally leaning on the support of certain power-ful, memorable phrases that stuck in his mind: 'O Mother of God, thou that lovest God and art full of grace. . .'. Then, in wordless prayer, he would return to the vaporous clouds, the mists swirling across the layers of his conscious-ness, which groaned and shifted like ice breaking up on the rivers in spring.

To express truly and completely the anguish which was burdening him, neither set prayers nor even his own words sufficed; the only means was to kneel upon aching knees (although he was now oblivious of the pain) and to gaze before him intently in silent devotion. This was the way he could lay before God the totality of his life and his present suffering. God must surely know that he had not spent his life in the service for the sake of personal glory or to wield power; the medals he wore were not mere adornments and he was praying for the success of his troops not in order to save his own reputation, but to serve the might of Russia, for much of her future destiny might depend upon this opening battle of the campaign.

He prayed that the victims of war might not die in vain; that there might be a reward for the sacrifice made by those who, struck down unawares by lead and iron, might not even have time to cross themselves before dying. He prayed for clarity to be granted to his anguished mind, so that on that crucial, topmost peak of time he might take the right decision – and thus ensure that those who gave their lives did not do so for nothing.

As he knelt, the full weight of his body pressing to the floor through his knees, he stared at the folding icon placed at the level of his eyes. Whispering, he prayed and crossed himself – and each time he did so the weight of his right arm seemed to grow less, the burden of his body seemed to lighten, and light filled his mind; soundlessly and invisibly the heaviness and darkness fell away from him, vanished, evaporated: God had taken all the burden upon Himself, for in him lay the power to give rest to all who were heavy-laden.

The strongest prayer of all is found where the individual is the most deprived. Solzhenitsyn himself, perhaps then in the process of becoming an Orthodox believer, experienced the force of Evangelical (Protestant) prayer while he was in a labour camp in the late 1940s and he represented this in the person of the Baptist, Alyosha, in a powerful passage in his largely autobiographical novel, *One Day in the Life of Ivan Denisovich*, his only major work published in the Soviet Union (1962). Alyosha says that, even in these conditions of utter deprivation, prayer must be for things of the spirit – for God to remove the 'scum of anger' from one's heart, for example – not for an improvement in the appalling physical conditions of life. Alyosha occupies only a few pages in the book, yet he stands out from the other characters as a hero, a Christian whose characteristics were laid before the public and read about by literally millions of people at the height of the Khrushchev persecution. The faith, it seems, will always cause atheists to pause and wonder, sometimes even bringing them to Christ. Solzhenitsyn gives us more than a hint that the barriers between the different traditions of the faith are likely one day to come down in the Soviet Union. Ecumenism begins not in the theological seminaries or the international church conference, but in the prison cell.

When we move on to the 1970s, we find prisoners, including the Orthodox, still harassed for their determination to keep their religious observations in prison. Ye. I. Pashnin-

Speransky told his story in a document which reached the West recently (published in *Religion in Communist Lands*, No. 4, 1977, pp. 264–6). The guards would systematically confiscate any piece of Christian literature which they could find in the camp. In June 1975 Pashnin-Speransky began a hunger-strike in protest against the confiscation of his hand-written prayer book and on that occasion it was returned the next day. Finding a place to pray undisturbed was always a problem. Even rising early to do so was treated as an offence punishable by withdrawal of all privileges: the right to buy goods at the camp shop and to receive food parcels. He and a friend found a store-room where they could pray, but the authorities found out and padlocked it. Then they resorted to praying together outside in sub-zero temperatures, but their discovery led to a further withdrawal of privileges. The Orthodox tradition demands corporate prayer, states Pashnin-Speransky, and he recounts how the believers resorted to a subterfuge to fulfil their obligations. They began to divide into groups of two or three, pretending to have conversations behind the barracks. By keeping their heads covered (against the tradition) they managed to conceal what they were doing and a priest among them gave special dispensation for this, provided they removed their hats momentarily to make the sign of the cross. Once three of them managed to slip away and to climb into a refrigerated lorry, where they immediately threw themselves on their knees and worshipped Christ. An attempt to come together for the traditional 'agape', the communal meal at Easter, was punished by confinement to an isolation cell. Any private letter home mentioning religion would be confiscated by the censorship.

Anatoli Levitin, whom we have already mentioned (see p. 24) was more fortunate. He was in prison for carrying out an informal religious educational programme for young people. His intransigence in prison led him to an isolation cell and here he was able to pray through the liturgy every day undisturbed. His account of this (here slightly abbreviated; for the full version see *Religion in Communist Lands*, No. 2, 1974, pp. 24–5) is one of the most impressive passages on prayer which it has ever been my privilege to read:

> The greatest miracle of all is prayer. I have only to turn my thoughts to God and I suddenly feel a force bursting into me; there is new strength in my soul, in my entire being. . . . The basis of my whole spiritual life is the Orthodox liturgy, so while I was in prison I attended it every day in my imagination. At 8.00 in the morning I would begin walking around my cell, repeating its words to myself. I was then inseparably linked to the whole Christian world. In the Great Litany I would always pray for the Pope and for the Oecumenical Patriarch, as well as for the leaders of my own church. At the central point of the liturgy . . . I felt myself standing before the face of the Lord, sensing almost physically his wounded, bleeding body. I would begin praying in my own words, remembering all those near to me, those in prison and those who were free, those still alive and those who had died. More and more names welled up from my memory. . . . The prison walls moved apart and the whole universe became my residence, visible and invisible, the universe for which that wounded, pierced body offered itself as a sacrifice. . . . After this, I experienced an exaltation of spirit all day – I felt purified within. Not only my own prayer helped me, but even more the prayer of many other faithful Christians. I felt it continually, working from a distance, lifting me up as though on wings, giving me living water and the bread of life, peace of soul, rest and love.

Here is true ecumenical prayer, in the sense both that it embraces the world and that all denominations can learn from it. One hopes that one day the ears of Christendom will be truly open to the message from the Russian Church. When they are, the hearers will find a world of rich experience within it.

5

The Perfect Way

When I went to the Soviet Union for the first time in 1959, although there were then many more official monasteries than there are now, I was probably not so far away from sharing the views of my co-students at Moscow University: monasticism is irrelevant to the twentieth century. My opinions have changed, changed primarily because of my encounter with Russia, but also with Romania, where over one hundred monasteries and convents shine as beacons in a materialistic world. Probably even then if I had been able to gain any real insight into the inner life of the Russian Church I would have thought differently. But for an outsider, especially a foreigner, it is almost as difficult to make this encounter with monasticism now as it was then. Gradually, however, my views changed by becoming acquainted with the emerging unpublished spiritual literature from the Soviet Union, and then by being a guest in 1978 of the Romanian Orthodox Church, observing the rich and developed spiritual life in many monasteries and convents.

The experience which first made me aware that I might have been making some error of judgement came in the mid-1960s, when I first read an unpublished article, 'Monasticism and the Modern World', which was written in 1963 by Anatoli Levitin, a – to me – unknown author, whom I would later come to know personally. He said:

> Monasticism is not an institution, foundation or a historical phenomenon, but an element, just as love, art and religion are elements. . . .
> 'Take this candle, brother, and see how yours must be

a pure and virtuous life, how you must be a light to the world through your exemplary morals.'

Thus speaks the abbot as he hands over a lighted candle to the newly-tonsured monk. . . .

At no time (even in the age of sputniks and cosmonauts) can debauchery, egotism and moral laxity be useful. Neither can atheism be, for it is an ideology which looks at the world as an arena of chaotic or moribund forces.

Always, at all times, the monastery has been the best school for educating people to clean living, self-denial and unselfishness. The monastery was the highest ideal for old Russia and it has remained so for many Russian people who have attained the peak of culture. . . .

Monasticism is an exaltation of man to the angels, a betrothal to purity. . . . It is an imitation of Christ. . . . It is not something sombre, sad or depressing. It is joy and eternal Easter (as we see it in the two great monks, St Seraphim of Sarov and St Francis of Assisi). . . . A monk is a fighter for truth, a soldier for Christ's cause, a manly and fearless warrior. . . .

We firmly believe in the coming of a new wave of monasticism in the Russian Church. The future of Russia is with the ardent and zealous young people of our country who, despite opposition, are every day attaining to the faith. New monks will come from among them – zealous warriors for Christ's cause. They will renew and transform the Church of Christ and the Russian land with their purity, self-sacrifice and spiritual ardour (quoted in my book, *Patriarch and Prophets*, pp. 87–90).

When I first read them, these words seemed strange, possibly even misguided, but they struck me with such force and obvious sincerity that I had to take notice of them. It would be much more difficult to reject them out of hand now. Indeed, they already seem prophetic, even though much that they say has not yet come to pass.

They were written at a time when the very existence of

monasticism in the Soviet Union was under severe physical threat. During the period of relative relaxation for the Orthodox Church after 1945 there had probably been about seventy monasteries and convents in existence. One of the prongs of Khrushchev's anti-religious campaign was to put an end to this 'aspect of religious life, which in any case was not guaranteed under Soviet law. The campaign succeeded in reducing this number to about sixteen (six monasteries and ten convents) confined almost entirely to the western area of the Soviet Union. Several of these came under severe threat and some of them (for example, Pochaev in the Western Ukraine, which we mentioned in the Introduction) remained open only as a result of the most determined local resistance, coupled with just enough publicity abroad to touch the sensitivity of the regime.

Some of the most venerated monasteries in the whole country were closed under Khrushchev, most notable among them perhaps being the Monastery of the Caves at Kiev. Since his day, efforts to reopen this and others have become increasingly persistent, but up to the time of writing they have remained without success. The rigidity of the authorities is probably to be explained more by the growing number of young people who would like to join them, rather than by their supposed irrelevance to modern life.

Father Gleb Yakunin, in his extended essay of 1979, 'The Present Situation of the Russian Orthodox Church', states that every single one of the monasteries open would contain more young people leading the religious life but for the *numerus clausus* operated by the authorities. The age-level is forced to remain artificially high, so that the monasteries seem to be little more than homes for the aged and invalids. It is virtually impossible for young people to gain acceptance as novices (though we should note that a very small number of theological students from the three seminaries eventually receive the tonsure, probably each one individually with state approval, so that the way is opened for him to become a bishop: married clergy remain as parish priests in the Orthodox Church, unless they become widowed). Monks who build up an especial following among pilgrims are often expelled from the monastery, while others have left semi-voluntarily because of the intolerable interference by the state in their lives.

A natural result of all this is that some of the most dedicated would-be monks and nuns give up the attempt to settle in an institution recognized by the state and secretly set up their own. Some churches, notably the Roman Catholic, are totally barred in the Soviet Union from having any monasteries whatsoever. The presence of unofficial monasteries merges into the continuing existence of the 'holy men' (*startsy*), whom we shall consider in the next chapter.

Despite the never-ending restraints upon them, the official monasteries continue to be more than just a magnet for pilgrims; they are still centres of deep and genuine renewal for the life of the Russian Orthodox Church. Even a foreign Russian speaker with the leisure to mingle among the pilgrims at the Holy Trinity Monastery, Zagorsk, is not likely to penetrate that deeply below the surface of what he is seeing.

Where the curtain is occasionally lifted for the outsider to see some glimpses of the spiritual reality behind the monastery or convent wall, the result is almost invariably impressive, giving a hint of the true spiritual depths which still exist. In her study of 'Monasticism in the Soviet Union' (*Religion in Communist Lands*, No. 1, 1976, pp. 28–34) Marite Sapiets describes the flourishing Convent of St Nicholas in Mukachevo, virtually inaccessible to foreigners in the foothills of the Carpathians in Western Ukraine. There are at present about one hundred and twenty nuns in residence. Mother Paraskeva, the last abbess before the present one, died in 1967. The influence she had in her later years and particularly on her deathbed is still a living reality among local people. She said in her testament which was read at her funeral:

I can no more address you with my lips and voice as before, because I have breath and speech failure. But my words come to you through this poor letter. The temple of my body has been destroyed and given to the earth according to the word of the Lord, 'Dust thou art and to dust shalt thou return'. But I look for the resurrection of the dead and I hope to inherit the age to come. Jesus Christ, my Lord and my God, is my hope and salvation. I have gone away from you on a long road, and I am walking along a path unknown to me. . . . But the time of Christ's second coming is approaching. . . . May God grant that we shall meet then.

In 1963, during Khrushchev's anti-religious campaign, an atheist activist, Gennadi Gerodnik, published a pamphlet in Moscow entitled *The Truth about the Monastery of the Caves at Pskov*. Though it contained the standard anti-religious terminology, this gave plenty of evidence of the vigorous religious life continuing there. The writer tells of the determined campaign by the monks, for example, to prevent incursions on to their territory by the new atheist guides appointed by the local authorities.

This work itself called forth a defence by Anatoli Levitin, one of the first *samizdat* documents on monasticism to reach the West (extracts published in English in my *Patriarch and Prophets*, pp. 93–7). Here is his portrait of the abbot, Archimandrite Alipi (who died in 1975):

He is a colourful and individual character. He is a real Russian, a native of the Moscow region, the son of a shepherd. As a layman, his name was Ivan Mikhailovich Voronov. At twenty he left the country, moved to the capital and became a labourer on the metro-building project. He worked days and nights, receiving thanks and awards. Then the war came and Ivan Mikhailovich went to the front, fighting throughout the four years and defending Moscow. He was wounded several times and awarded orders and medals.

After the war he stopped to think. He thought for long and sought the truth. He went to the Baptists and other sects, but finally entered a seminary and the monastery.

For a long time, in peasant fashion, he tried it out and finally took the irrevocable step.

He works night and day at physical labour: hewing wood, carrying planks, breaking ice, painting, whitewashing, cleaning. He makes everyone else work, too. He is a talented man, a good artist. He is a brave warrior, defending the monastery resolutely and courageously. If the need arose, he would die for it.

To look at him you would think he was a thickset peasant, bearded and coarse; he is a real abbot, though – strict but just, capable of anger, but humane.

He reminisces pleasantly about his mother; he talks in a tender, sincere and good way with people and he is obviously compassionate towards them.

I have been at his services and heard his sermons. He officiates with feeling and preaches with conviction. I have talked with him several times. He looks at me and my writings with a certain amazement, I feel. I am one of the old-styled intelligentsia, apparently not comprehensible to him.

Not even Anatoli Levitin, as an outsider, albeit one completely sympathetic to the monastic tradition, conveys the full spiritual depth to be found in today's Russian monasteries. This can best be found in a *samizdat* book, entitled *A Short History of the Monastery of the Caves at Pskov*, which reached the West in the early 1970s. Here is part of the anonymous introduction to that book, reprinted from *Religion in Communist Lands*, No. 1, 1976, pp. 45–7.

A monk is a son who has come to himself, for whom all the past, present and future have blended into one and turned into an endlessly long moment of the sweetest self-oblivion on the Father's breast. . . . The cry of his penitent prayer is still on his lips, but his heart – his heart has long ago heard the answer with its own cry, a cry of joy at sinking into the unfathomable abyss of God's total forgiveness and mercy! . . .

As a man ignorant of music cannot completely understand and enjoy its harmonious, delicate sounds, so a man who is ignorant of God, who denies religion, cannot understand the true meaning of monasticism. The elevated feelings of the ascetic who has found in his soul the Kingdom of Heaven and who bears the Living God within himself are beyond his comprehension. Music delights our ears and calls forth a noble feeling — a feeling of joy and enthusiasm, but religion, that is, the Spirit of God, by the rays of his blessing and love delights the whole of our being, calling forth indescribable rapture and tender emotion. Therefore this feeling is still greater, more exalted and more noble, and one should not show mere curiosity and trifle with religion. On the contrary, one should reach out after this noble feeling. When we pray, God's rays of blessing descend upon us, and not only our hearing but all our feelings are sanctified: sight, smell, taste, touch — a man's whole being, and then man himself is ennobled.

When you hear a moving song or speech you hold your breath, your heart stops beating and you stand as if transfixed, fearing the least rustle. This is precisely how, with breath held and heart stilled towards everything external, we must turn to God, who announces his presence in our hearts with the sweet words of the Spirit and with mellowed feelings.

How much colour and poetry, how much depth of feeling, what power of tender emotion is concealed in the hymns, canons and other canticles of the church! And rituals and ceremonies. They are a whole ocean containing every kind of treasure, consolation and delight. Life with all its anxieties and yearnings is so empty and soulless without them.

In order to know God one needs neither wealth nor learning, but one must be obedient and self-controlled, possess a humble spirit and love one's neighbour, and the Lord will love such a soul and will reveal himself to it and teach it love and humility, and will give it all that is needful, so that it may find peace in God.

Although the very aim of monasticism is the renewal by the Holy Spirit of the person who has become a monk, the holy Fathers suggest that the way of this aim is by penitence and humility, by reaching the point of weeping for oneself, and praying in affliction, by revealing so much sinfulness in oneself that one's conscience will bear testimony that we are subject servants in need of mercy.

The true way to God is found in a sense of deep faith, of filial, most humble obeisance before the Lord, of complete, heartfelt contrition, repentance and the fulfilling of all the commandments, without any examination of good works and spiritual victories, and with constant glorification and thanksgiving to the Lord and a thirst for blessed communion with him – the Only One. Sins and illnesses which occur will only deepen saving penitence and humility. Then men together with the psalmist will call out to God in joyful weeping: 'Blessed am I for thou hast chastened me'.

Even more personal and heartfelt is one of the chapters in this *Short History*. Had this been written by a Protestant in slightly different terminology, one would call it one of the classic descriptions of the 'born-again' experience. We reprint it here from *Religion in Communist Lands*, No. 6, 1974, pp. 18–21:

I have been made so infinitely rich with an abundance of heavenly treasures given to me by God that I am not able to count them. I am now a monk, however strange that may be, however incomprehensible. New attire, a new name, a new feeling which I had never known nor experienced before, a new inner peace, a new mood, everything is new – the whole of me has been made new.

Oh, what a glorious, supernatural action of grace! It has completely melted me, completely transformed me. You understand me, my dear, as the former Nicholas. (How I dislike repeating my worldly name.) He no longer exists, he has completely disappeared; he was taken somewhere and buried deep in the earth, so that not even the smallest trace remains. Sometimes I have a desire to picture the former Nicholas, but no, it never works; my imagination is stretched to its limit, but I can never imagine the the former Nicholas. It is as if I fell into a deep sleep. . . . Then, roused from it, I look round, I want to recall what happened before I was lost in sleep but I cannot remember my previous condition, as if someone had wiped it from my consciousness and in place of my former condition had put something new, something completely new. Only a new present remained, one hitherto unknown to me, and a distant future.

A child born into the world does not remember its life in the womb. That is what I am like. Thanks to taking monastic vows, I felt like a baby and now I cannot remember my secular life. It is as if I have now been born into the world and all the past has become a dream. Isolated recollections of the past, fragments are preserved but not the former essence of my being; my soul has become completely different.

I will tell you how I gradually approached my present state – or rather how God's grace gradually drew me to it. To remember this is also useful for me personally, for it strengthens, encourages and inspires me. In moments of musing on the transitory nature of all things worldly, an awareness that you have dedicated yourself to the service of the Lord God, that you belong to no other than him, can provide a flow of fresh strength for future spiritual feats, can encourage and make one spiritually happy. A sign of such happiness is love of God and one's neighbour; in the attainment of humility, not to notice when you are offended, hurt and humiliated is also a sign.

From the age of eight, by the inscrutable paths of the Most High Providence, the grace of God was calling me to that exalted end – to a monastic life, but I only took monastic vows considerably later. Many holy Fathers who have experienced a call and the moment of conversion have found difficulty in describing the ways in which God leads man. No less a danger awaits me, as I try to communicate

in words what defies description, to express in everyday
concepts what cannot be contained by them. Looking stead-
ily at the past, I can firmly tell you, my friend, that time
has not wiped away the indelible; on the contrary, it has
polished it, revealing the secret action of Divine Providence.
It is made manifest in everything: through the formation
of my character (due to the influence of specially designed
circumstances), the development of spiritual qualities, and
also through the appearance of one persistent thought – to
find the true meaning of life. In my soul, the process of
inner maturing for my new life was completed in a way
which is beyond understanding. I felt the invisible hand of
the Great Artist drawing heavenly images in my heart by
the grace of the Holy Spirit, images which drew me towards
a new life. My heart was filled with the hidden action of
God's grace. And from here I heard the wonderful sounds
of heavenly harmony, from here the stern voice of denunciation sounded, pointing to my unworthiness and sinfulness. Here in my heart a fierce struggle began between the
new and the old man. Mysterious states, which I had never
experienced before, took hold of my being. My reason was
puzzled. 'What is happening to me?' Often under the influence of passions my reason rebelled against those new
things my heart was experiencing, inflicting blow after blow
at my heart with lightning speed. But my poor heart, fighting and suffering, believed. In moments of exhaustion, it
felt the mysterious power of grace flowing into it, transforming the bitterness of suffering into a source of unearthly
joy. The Holy Spirit, the Comforter himself, revealed his
power in weakness. Then my proud mind was humbled,
recognizing the greatness of the spiritual world revealed to
it.

Such, my friend, are the true reasons which led me to
my new life. I do not think they are convincing for everyone,
in the same way as the mysteries of the spiritual world are
not revealed to everyone. I do not consider it necessary to
trouble you with a chronological account of the events of

my life, therefore I shall proceed to the most fundamental: an account of my feelings when I took monastic vows.

On entering the Monastery of St Sergius it was suggested that I ask for permission to become a monk. It was arranged that I take monastic vows on 25 October (old calendar) 1948, during the all-night vigil, on the eve of the Feast of the Holy Martyr Dmitri Solunsky (Mirotochivy). I went to confession. After confession I attended the whole liturgy, went to my cell and experienced something which one only knows perhaps on the verge of death. The clock in the monastery struck mid-day. A few hours more and the ceremony must begin. Oh, if you only knew how precious each minute was to me, how I tried not vainly to lose these minutes. I filled them with prayer, with thought and with reading the holy Fathers. I read, thought and remembered especially the words of the holy Fathers: of St Sergius of Radonezh, Serafim of Sarov, Archpriest John of Kronstadt, Ieroskhimonakh (priest-monk and solitary) Ambrose of Optina, Bishop Theofan the Hermit.*

It is said that a man may involuntarily recall the whole of his past life. So it was with me; in one moment my entire life rose before me in clear pictures. And what did I feel? What did I experience? God alone knows. . . . The self-sufficient world will never in any way understand these experiences, unless it is touched by the grace of God.

Before the light broke through to me, I began to experience an agony of soul – what a terrible agony it is fearful to recall. It was some kind of total depression as if something was sucking my heart, oppressing me, gnawing at me; something dark and hopeless – and nowhere was there help, nowhere consolation. It will be like this again only before death. The devil was fighting his last and most fearful battle. And, believe me, if it had not been for God's help, I would not have endured it. But the Lord is always

* Some of the saints and holy men of the Russian Orthodox Church, representing centuries from the fourteenth to the present, whose works are among the classics of Orthodox spirituality.

close to man. He watches the struggle and the moment he sees that man is exhausted immediately sends his gracious help. Thus in the most decisive moments I too was allowed to experience a sense of being completely abandoned, but then suddenly support was given to me. My soul was filled with unusual tenderness and grace-given warmth: in utter exhaustion I fell face downwards before the holy icon and began to weep sweet tears. Overjoyed and in rapture I began to read the Gospel.

A bell chimed, indicating the beginning of the evening service. After a short prayer in my cell to the Saviour and to the Mother of God, tenderness filled my soul. If you only knew what happened to me. . . . There was a quiet knock at the door of my cell. A monk entered, saying: 'The time has come, let us go.' I rose and once more, together with the monk, prayed to the Saviour and to the Mother of God, and bowed to the Saviour, the Mother of God and the icon of St Nicholas the Miracle-worker.

We went into the church. It was dark in the entrance to the church, the icon-lamps were flickering quietly. I remained alone at the side where the icon-stand was, separated by a curtain; there was an icon of the Saviour on the stand, with a candle burning before it. On a small table I saw a hair-shirt, stockings. . . . I had to change. I took off all my old clothes, discarding the old man, and, having put on a hair-shirt, took the form of the new man. Dressed in the hair-shirt and stockings, I stood throughout vespers behind the curtain in front of the icon of the Saviour. With longing and faith I gazed at the Divine Face; and he, Jesus Christ, gentle and meek of heart, looked at me. It was good then: peaceful and joyous. You look down at yourself – you are completely white, the hair-shirt down to your ankles, you stand unclothed, aware of your insignificance before your Creator. You fall before the icon, seize your head in your hands . . . and sink into contemplation of God . . . 'Holy Lord', the choir sings for the last time, softly and smoothly as at a funeral, 'Holy and Strong, Holy and

71

Eternal, have mercy on us.' With measured solemn steps a host of monks drew near me, dressed in *klobuki* (monk's head-dress) and long robes, with candles alight in their hands; they came up to me and led me to the dais before the iconostasis. The Father Archimandrite, the superior of the monastery, stood in front of the royal gates beside the icon-stand with a cross and a Gospel.

'Oh Father, open thou thine arms to me', the choir sang softly and mournfully.

Covered in robes, I entered the sanctuary and prostrated myself, touching the very floor with my face; I stretched out my arms in the form of a cross; I do not remember very well what happened, everything grew very dim . . . I fell again. . . . Suddenly, when I was lying on the dais, I heard the special reading, given at the taking of the vows. 'God is merciful, like a Father who loves his children. Child, he sees your humility and genuine repentance and he accepts you after you have repented like the prodigal son, when you fall before him in sincerity of heart.'

The Father Archimandrite came up to me and raised me to my feet. Then I made publicly, before the face of God, the magnificent and difficult monastic vows. After that they clothed me in a monk's habit, putting on my shoulders a black *paraman* with a white cross; around it were written the marvellous words: 'For I bear in my body the marks of the Lord Jesus'. At times I feel these words so strongly. On my breast they placed a wooden cross as an eternal reminder of the suffering and destruction, the humiliation, the abuse and insults, the crucifixion and death of our Lord Jesus Christ. I was dressed in a cassock; a leather belt was put round my waist; then I was clothed in a mantle and *klobuk*. Then they handed me a burning candle and a wooden cross.

Thus I was buried for the sake of the world. I died and moved into a spiritual world, although physically I still remain on the earth. What I felt and experienced when, dressed as a monk, I stood at the iconostasis before the icon of the Saviour, with a cross and a candle in my hand, defies description. My soul felt that in Jesus Christ was hidden the source of eternal blessing. And the aim of the monastic life is to be a participant in these heavenly blessings through continually calling on the saving name of our Lord Jesus Christ. For five days and five nights I did not leave the church, every day I partook of the holy sacraments of Christ. During that time I pondered over and underwent so much which I will probably never again experience during the rest of my life. Everything was there: the bliss of heaven and the agony of hell; but chiefly bliss.

While such depths exist within the Russian Orthodox Church, it will continue not only to attract people, especially the young, within the Soviet Union, but its spirituality will form a significant passage in the record of twentieth-century Christianity.

6

Startsy: The Secret Inspiration

When the persecution has been at its worst, when the Church has had to go underground to survive at all, the *starets* (plural: *startsy*) has not had basically to adapt his role in order to continue as the spiritual dynamo of the Russian Orthodox Church, the inspiration of the people. The 'holy man' (literally 'elder'), quite outside the formal structures of the ecclesiastical establishment, does not need to officiate, to visit parishioners, to organize anything. He just needs to be. Wherever he is, deep in hiding in the forests, in a side-street, anywhere, people will find him and send others to him. That is where he often was in the nineteenth century, avoiding the crowding influence of a changing society and ignoring any official favours which came the Church's way. That is where he is now. If he is found and put behind barbed wire, his new circle of spiritual children will be those sharing his barracks or cell. It is to the *starets* more than anything that the Russian Orthodox Church owes its enormous staying-power.

I remember a few years ago visiting the home of one of the most active and respected parish priests in Moscow, a man who had had his difficulties with the authorities, had ridden them out with fortitude and was still bringing spiritual enlightenment literally to thousands. I asked how he, as a very old man, coped with the immense pressures upon him and was amazed at his reply. He took his spiritual direction from a *starets*, a hermit whom he rarely saw, but with whom he corresponded regularly. I was never again tempted to undervalue the role of the holy man.

The origin of the tradition of the *starets* is obscured by the mists of medieval Russian Christian history. The power of

74

the despot was controlled and humanized by the holy men, who were not members of their court, living genuinely ascetic lives far from the seat of power, but nevertheless being visited from time to time by the ruler when he was under stress and in need of guidance. The *starets* would in no way compromise his basic Christian message because it was the Tsar who came to see him. A genuine relationship would develop the more easily because of the self-abnegation of the former who was totally without personal ambition and never curried favour for advancement. Such a man, for example, was St Sergius of Radonezh, who became virtually the patron saint of Russia. As friend and adviser to Prince Dmitri Donskoi in the fourteenth century, he wielded tremendous personal influence, but he lived his life in the depths of the forests 'beyond the hills', which is what Zagorsk means, a distance which modern communications have eaten up, but was very real and even hazardous to the medieval traveller. His monastery stands as a magnificent living monument today, encompassing not only a rich complex of churches, but also a functioning monastery, theological academy and seminary.

After many years of neglect, the monastery of Optina Pustyn was rebuilt in 1796. It soon became the most famous place of spiritual refuge in Russia, not because it was accessible or favoured by the hierarchy – rather the opposite. There was a succession of *startsy* there throughout the nineteenth century, some well known, some less so, ready at all times to receive pilgrims from all over Russia. No one was ever turned away. They did not put the 'spiritual' into its own separate compartment. They were just as ready to advise the peasant on how to farm his strip of land or to calm the latest dispute between neighbours as to give the parish priest the kind of advice still being offered a century later in the way described above.

Nearly all the great authors of the nineteenth century made their way there at one time or other, some, like Tolstoy, who lived five days' walk away at Yasnaya Polyana, frequently. Dostoevsky partly modelled his compelling portrait of Father

Zosima in the *The Brothers Karamazov* on the *starets* Amvrosy of Optina Pustyn.

So great was the spiritual power of the *starets* considered to be in old Russia that people thought he had the power to look directly into their souls, laying open before themselves and God both the good and the evil. It is said of St John of Kronstadt, who died in 1908, that if people in St Petersburg saw him coming along the street they would cross to the other side if they had anything on their conscience, even if they were completely unknown to him, so that he should not look into their eyes.

The Revolution of 1917, as carried through by Stalin, completely destroyed the Church as a structure. The visible organization of administration, dioceses, monasteries, theological seminaries, even of over ninety per cent of the parishes, was all swept away. Apart from a handful of priests who somehow managed to remain at their posts, the clergy were virtually liquidated. Many thousands died. The rest were exiled or engulfed by the prison camps, the network of which grew to monstrous size under Stalin. The survival of the Church under these conditions, leading to its revival after the Second World War and its growth among young people today, is a miracle, a miracle which can be explained chiefly by the way the *startsy* preserved the essentials of the faith during the catclysm. They guarded its purity, sometimes even managing to impart it to others while the storm raged around them.

Such conditions even created new *startsy*. There were 'worldly' priests who lost all, family, house, church, congregation, yet faced the terror with a strengthened faith which they scarcely knew they possessed. Such a man was Father Pavel, whom we have already described in Chapter 1.

Exiles who survived longer and with more strength than Father Pavel (he died in 1932) often established some kind of underground organization, being especially motivated to do so after Metropolitan Sergius, the senior church leader remaining at liberty, had come to a compromise agreement with the state in 1927. Under various names, such as the 'True Orthodox Church' and the 'Orthodox Christian Wanderers', the faith survived, not only in the remote countryside, but also to some extent in the towns. That pure spiritual source still injects its vitality into the veins of the Russian Church today. Soviet power manages only barely to touch such people, though from time to time there is news of the exposure and destruction of an underground monastery. One wonders how many dozens exist for every one that is discovered.

One of the most recent examples was in the Abkhazian Autonomous Republic in 1976. According to the local newspaper, wrote the Reuter correspondent Robert Evans (*Berichte, Glaube in der 2 Welt*, October 1976, pp. 6–7), the leader of the True Orthodox Church in the area, Father Grigori Sekach, established a whole network of underground monasteries and churches. The priest was sentenced to four years' imprisonment for having drawn many young people into these activities as monks and nuns. He moved to this area from Ukraine in 1964, said the report, drawn by the former splendour of the great monastery Novy Afon (New Athos) closed in 1924 after the advent of Soviet power in the region. Sekach allegedly travelled far and wide to recruit new candidates to bring back to his religious institutions. We do not know enough about this monk to say whether or not he was a true *starets*, but the ready influence he had on others suggests that he was.

The majority of *startsy* keep their activities on a quieter level; therefore we tend to hear less about them. Nevertheless, from scattered sources one can build up a picture. Father Nikon is a typical as anyone can be of the *starets* of the twentieth century. He died almost twenty years ago, in 1963, during the time of the Khrushchev persecution, and remained almost totally unknown outside his own circle, not only in the West, but also in the Soviet Union, until a volume of his spiritual writings appeared in the original language in Paris in 1979, under the title *Letters to My Spiritual Children*. It is to

77

Nikita Struve's introduction that I am indebted for this information about him.

Nikolai Nikolaevich Borovyov, as Nikon was called before he took his monastic name, was born at Bezhetsk, north of Tver, into a humble family in 1894. At school (his curriculum illustrates how enlightened provincial education could be at the time) he showed an early and outstanding talent in just about every direction: music, art, maths, foreign languages. On leaving school he began studying to be a doctor in St Petersburg. It was at this time that the course of his life underwent a dramatic change. Originally full of belief in the power of science to improve the lot of the human race, he came to believe during his first year of study that total devotion to the Christian faith would help him the more directly to serve his fellow-men. He left the institute and began a lonely ascetic life, studying the Gospels and the church Fathers. Here, indeed, he did feel that he was finding something of much more lasting value for human existence than he had done in his earlier studies.

He joined the Moscow Theological Seminary at the age of twenty-four in the very year of the Revolution, 1917, but had to leave two years later with his studies uncompleted, as the Bolsheviks closed down the institute. Deprived once again of a clear direction in life, Nikolai found his way to Sukhnichi in Belorussia. He spent no less than ten years there reading, studying and praying more or less in secret seclusion. In 1931 he took monastic vows in Minsk, his new name, Nikon, being a symbol of the 'victory' of the Church which was by then undergoing persecution to the point of extinction. Two years to the day after receiving the tonsure he was discovered, arrested and eventually sent to Siberia for four years.

After the Second World War parishes began to reopen, so Nikon, now aged fifty-one, was able for the first time in his life to begin pastoral work at Kozelsk, south of Kaluga. Already he was in trouble because of the attention his sermons were attracting. To prevent his building up too great a local following, the authorities secured his rapid removal to three other towns in succession, followed finally by his being sent to a tiny and impoverished congregation at Gzhatsk, a hundred miles west of Moscow.

It was there that he accomplished the real work of his life. Despite the remoteness of the place, people began to come to him in hordes. He was even forbidden to receive visitors. Here he learned what he called 'original humility': he came to realize that 'we have nothing of our own, living solely from the grace of God'.

His letters demonstrate a strong faith, firmly rooted in the practical concerns of the people. Their spiritual profundity is achieved not out of simplicity, but from years of preparation followed by physical suffering. His advice is unfailingly to the point, addressed to the individual in a situation where he is in deep need of counsel. For example, in his letter 'On Despair' he writes:

> You beg me to write to you. A drowning man clutches at a straw, so you seek help among those close to you in your state of spiritual agitation. My experience of life has led me to the view that no one can help us, neither ourselves, nor other people, but only the Lord. Not only is your spiritual state failing to improve, but it is even becoming unbearable at times because you have so little hope in God. You look at your sins and justly consider that you will have to suffer for them in the life to come and even here before death, where you will undergo many trials.
>
> Such an attitude is likely to lead you into complete despair. Can that really happen to a Christian? If a man can save himself by his own virtue, then why did the Lord Jesus Christ have to suffer? No one has entered the Kingdom of God as a result of his own merit (*Nadezhda* [Hope] 1, pp. 219–20).

On 'Drunkenness' Nikon writes something which the Soviet authorities might, with benefit, copy to help them in their current campaign against this vice which is occupying so much attention in the Soviet press at the moment:

I hear that you are continuing to have a good drink, to your own extreme harm. What lies in waiting for a man along this road? I'll tell you right now. If you don't combat this ailment, you'll fall completely into the power of devils. They will push you to drink more and more and as a result your nervous system will be upset. You will become irascible. Arguments which begin over trivialities will become more and more bitter and prolonged. You won't have enough money, you'll lose your job, you'll have to sell your possessions and get humiliatingly into debt; perhaps you'll even have to steal. Your anger will increase to a Satanic fury; you'll even feel an urge to kill (*Nadezhda* 1, p. 210).

Father Tavrion Batozsky was another man of God who never achieved anything in life from the point of view of the world, yet died in August 1978 at the age of eighty as a revered, and in his way influential, figure. Unlike Father Nikon, he never had any other ideal in life except to be a monk. So great was this pull and so early did he feel it that he ran away from his home near Kharkov in Ukraine to the Glinsk Monastery as a young boy and by the time he was thirteen (1911) his father had reluctantly given him permission to live there permanently. There is so much evidence that, before the cataclysm hit the Russian Orthodox Church in 1917, God was preparing a generation of people of extraordinary toughness to withstand what was to come. Father Tavrion was one of those. He was ordained four years after the Revolution and in 1928, when he was thirty, he began the central part of his life, twenty-eight years of unbroken imprisonment and exile, during which he suffered untold deprivations and tortures. The ostensible reason for his arrest was that he had taken part in the secret election of a successor to Patriarch Tikhon.

In 1957 Father Tavrion was able to return once more, now as abbot, to his beloved Glinsk Monastery, where he had begun his religious life forty-six years previously. Far from wishing to take life a little easier after all the pain he had undergone, he introduced a new regime, with greater emphasis on prayer and fasting. Such a return to monastic first principles was not universally to the liking of the monks under him. They managed successfully to petition his superiors for his removal and he stayed there only eighteen months.

This served only to enhance his spiritual authority, however, and wherever he went during a succession of rapid moves during the Khrushchev persecution people flocked to hear him preach and to seek his counsel. While in the village of Nekous in 1964, Metropolitan Ioann Wendland banned him from preaching because the great flood of believers coming into his church was offending the authorities.

In 1969 Father Tavrion moved to Latvia, where he finally achieved almost a decade of settled existence as spiritual counsellor of the Transfiguration Convent near Jelgava. Pilgrims from all over the Soviet Union began to visit him there and his saintly personality seemed to have an especial attraction for the young. In the words of a *samizdat* memoir published about him in the West soon after his death:

> Faithful to the ancient Russian monastic tradition, he became not only spiritual father of the convent, but also an efficient administrator, a 'builder and decorator'. Every year new hospices for pilgrims grew up. The convent, until then little known and in a poor state of repair, able to accommodate barely twenty guests at a meal, was transformed into a place of pilgrimage, bursting with tens of thousands of believers from every part of the country. Drawn by tales of this extraordinary *starets*, they flocked from the spiritual desert of modern life as to a fount of 'living water'; the sick, the old, intellectuals from the big cities, peasants, engineers, hippies, all the suffering people. . . . Today in summer you will find about two hundred people every day. . . .

> 'Very early in the morning, just before five when the city is still asleep, there is such beauty here when we sing the Gloria and gather at the banquet of the Lamb of God',

says the *starets*. Nowhere have I seen the liturgy celebrated with such humility and gentleness, with such conviction and authority, such paschal joy. One can really feel the strength of the prayers of the *starets*, the fire of the Spirit in it.

At every liturgy there is a sermon – often two or three – which is like a torrent of life-giving wisdom, like a judgement before the throne of God, laying bare the secrets of our conscience, but bathing our heart with the great love and tenderness of the heavenly Father. What strikes one most is that it is not just the priest and choir who sing; everyone joins in. Many young people from Moscow have learnt here for the first time how to sing the psalms and services correctly. The vigorous exhortation of the *starets*: 'Come on, let us sing together, all of us!' remains for ever in the memory and draws a response from everyone. We must all let ourselves be transfigured by the Holy Spirit, rise from the dead, and join the Archimandrite in prayers for all mankind; we rise from Golgotha towards the Saviour. His sermons are splendid. They recall every Christian to true penitence. When for the first time I saw the *starets* preaching with his eyes closed and a Gospel in his hands, I felt that such sweetness, humility and power could dwell only in a saint. Many have felt the charismatic effect of the sermons to be a reply to their most insoluble personal problems, to perplexity, error and doubt.

To put across his teaching in brief, one could say that the word of God, Holy Communion and prayer and the heroic strength of his faith are at the same time both a probing judgement and love (*Russia Cristiana*, Milan, No. 168, November–December 1979).

Another memoir of Father Tavrion which has come to hand is a striking account of the atmosphere in the church belonging to the convent on the day he died, written by a woman whom he was counselling following her divorce, of which he was deeply critical. This was included in the Christian *sam-*

izdat journal, *Nadezhda*, No. 4. Included in the same volume is a short series of extracts from his sermons, remarkable for their practical application, especially the passage of instruction to parents on the Christian upbringing of their children.

Startsy, though withdrawn from the world, seem to have a role greater than ever in modern Soviet life and their personalities are now beginning to shine through the pages, often unpublished, of modern Russian Christian literature.

PART III

The Other Faiths

7

Conversion and the Camps

One day a book will be written on religion in the Soviet prison camps. It will show that when a human being is systematically deprived of everything which is normally considered his by right – family, home, work, a basic diet – at that very time the influence of the Christian faith is at its most powerful. One of the miracles of the twentieth century, yet to be described in detail, is the way that the Christian Church, driven completely off the public scene in the Soviet Union in the late 1920s and '30s, managed not only to survive underground, but also to revive. One could already fill many pages with stories of how people imprisoned for criminal activities had encounters in the closed conditions of the prison cell with men and women put there because of their Christian witness. Of course, many others besides criminals were also influenced in those conditions by the faith. When one learns of the quality of the witness, this goes some way towards explaining the effect it has had on thousands, perhaps hundreds of thousands, of people.

One of the most unforgettable Christian scenes in the prison-camp literature is in the last chapter of a book written by a communist and an atheist, not, as far as we know, converted by the incident she describes, though she admits it kept up her morale. Evgenia Ginzburg's *Into the Whirlwind* was published in 1967, describing the events of thirty years before. One of the important points it makes is that it was not only deviants, whether political, moral or criminal, who were swept away into the camps by Stalin's terror, but countless loyal members of the Communist Party, too, of which she was one.

The author describes the arrival of Easter in late April of the year in question, but Siberia held its winter savagely. On Easter Day itself a group of women from Voronezh, imprisoned for their Orthodox faith, asked to be dispensed from work that day. The camp officials ordered them out to do their slave labour in the forest regardless and they were driven by the rifle butts of the guards. When they arrived at the clearing where they were to do their logging, they dropped their axes and saws, sat down on the tree trunks and began to sing the Easter liturgy. The guards rounded them up, marched them out on to the ice covering one of the pools in the forest and made them take their boots off. Barefoot, they stood their ground on the thin film of water covering the ice and recited every syllable of the liturgy, while the other prisoners besought the guards not to be so brutal to these harmless people. Evgenia Ginzburg comments on the episode:

> Was this fanaticism, or fortitude in defence of the rights of conscience? Were we to admire them or regard them as mad? And, most troubling of all, should we have had the courage to act as they had? In the heat of the argument we forgot our hunger and exhaustion and the stinking dampness of the punishment-cell. It is a remarkable fact that not one of the women who had stood for so long on the ice went sick. As for the norm, next day they reached 120 per cent (*Into the Whirlwind*, p. 313).

In chapter four we discussed Solzhenitsyn's experience of ecumenical prayer in the prison camp and the influence which the Baptist, Alyosha, had on him. An equally remarkable, though much less known, example of something similar is to be found in the sermons of Father Dmitri Dudko, preached in the seventies in Moscow when he was free to do so and before the KGB began their systematic campaign to break him physically and mentally. These sermons were collected together and published in New York in English, under the title, *Our Hope*.

Father Dmitri made his sermons relevant by encouraging

written questions to be sent in, selected ones of which he would then answer, after grouping them together in themes. He further asked young people to send in their own experiences of how they became converted to the Christian faith. One reply, which he quoted at length in a sermon, read in part:

The members of my family are deeply atheistic by disposition. Even my grandmother and grandfather were non-believers. From childhood I learned my lesson well: that God was just a fable invented by ignorant people. The very word 'religion' evoked dark associations in me. I imagined emaciated faces with mindless eyes, dark, vaulted rooms, candles, tombs. . . .

Nothing made me really happy. Nothing was pleasant. I started to drink. You get drunk and things get a little easier. The longer it went on, the longer it took me to get really smashed. And so it went on. . . . I had already become an alcoholic of sorts. On my days off I'd drink myself unconscious . . . I got drunk, got into a fight and found myself in jail under Article 206.2 ('hooliganism').

There was another person in my cell, a Baptist, who prayed a great deal and would always cross himself before meals. Many people – including me – mocked him for this. Out of boredom I more or less dragged him into a dispute over religion. At first I just let my words run away with me, interspersing facetious comments about how old women just invented God. He answered every one of my flippant arguments seriously. His unshakeable conviction that he was correct began to irritate me. Soon, just for the fun of it, I began defending atheism seriously, proving by any means at my disposal that God could not exist.

I really could not have cared less about either God or atheism. I just wanted to break his confidence – that was the main thing. Arrogance pushed me on. And I achieved what I wanted. My cell-mate stopped talking. After a silence he began to cry, praying that his faith would be strengthened.

I felt no satisfaction in my victory. A horrible weight fell upon me. I felt sick, as though I had done something mean to someone. And he just kept on praying, but more calmly now. Suddenly he looked at me and smiled. I was amazed at his face: there was something joyous about it, pure, as though it had just been washed clean. The weight immediately fell from my soul. I understood that he had forgiven me. And then a light of some sort penetrated me, and I understood that God existed. It was not even so much that I understood, but rather I sensed it with my whole being. He is everywhere. He is our Father! We are his children, brothers one to another. I forgot that I was in prison and felt only one thing – a great joy and thankfulness to the Lord who had revealed himself to me, who was unworthy.

After this a strange and radiant thing happened to me. As a non-believer, I had read the holy Scriptures, but had always hit upon the 'dark' and 'incomprehensible'. For me the Scriptures were a fabric of contradictions. After I came to believe, each word of the Gospel was filled with meaning for me, close to my mind and heart (*Our Hope*, pp. 211–13, translation adapted).

It is rare indeed to find an Orthodox priest so willing to give public testimony to the beneficial influence of someone of the Protestant faith. Usually positive ecumenical action is confined to the official sending of separate Orthodox and Baptist delegations to the World Council of Churches meetings, or at home to participating in government-sponsored 'peace' meetings. It is even rarer to find an Orthodox preacher ready to talk openly of prison experience and to give evidence of conversion while undergoing it. The Soviet authorities aim consistently to silence such testimony and in Father Dmitri's case, seven years after the sermon quoted, they seem to have done so. He was not only removed from his parish, but badly injured in a car accident which was probably an attempt on his life. Both his legs were broken. Later he was arrested and imprisoned, then was forced to make some kind of false confession before being released in 1980, a seemingly broken man. Nevertheless, Father Dmitri's preaching has brought thousands to Christ and this work lives on in his disciples, whatever the spiritual torments he himself is now suffering.

One of the most moving stories to come out of the prison camps in recent years is that of Vasili Kozlov, a criminal who became a Christian in a Soviet prison. His story, addressed to the Soviet leadership, is so impressive that to retell it could only dim its impact, so here it is in his own words, with just a few abbreviations, now told in book form for the first time:

I, Vasili Ivanovich Kozlov, was born in 1924 in the village of Cherly, Takanysh District, in the Tartar Autonomous Republic, into the family of a poor peasant. By nationality I am Russian.

My father died in 1933. We were five children left alone without a father and we had to fend for ourselves. I was tempted out on to the streets and I committed a theft, so at fifteen I landed up in prison with a big sentence for a boy – four years. Far from being reformed by imprisonment at such an age, I was confirmed in my wickedness.

In 1943, after being set free, I was sent to the front and within a year was seriously wounded in the chest. After hospital and a short period of convalescence I was sent back again into the army. In 1945 I was demobilized and again returned to my criminal life, so that in 1946 I was condemned to five years' imprisonment for having a firearm in my possession.

Thus I lived without God and without morals and would not give up my criminal life. In 1947, in the camp itself, I was given an additional sentence for committing acts of gangsterism in the camp: ten years.

Sometimes I fell into despair, looking for a way out of the situation I was in. Life had no interest whatsoever for me. I tried everything I could to end my life, and yet I wanted to live, but not in this way. I started to define the reason for the tragedy of my life.

I now know the reason for my fall: I was born in 1924 and even while I was sitting at my school desk, I was constantly told that there was no God. And if there is no belief in God, then there are no morals either. This was the path of the soul's destruction and the way to moral and physical degeneration.

But among prisoners I happened to see other people who did have good morals and high ideals in life. These were Christians, believers. They had been sentenced and put among criminals for their living faith in God.

I confessed that I was being punished deservedly: for theft, robbery and violence. But these people had been given far greater sentences of twenty or twenty-five years' imprisonment for their faith.

Among the general despair, while prisoners like myself were cursing ourselves, cursing the camp, the authorities and everything in the world, while we were slitting open our veins and stomachs or hanging ourselves, the Christians did not despair.

Life in the camp in these harsh conditions did not dismay them. They were shining with a spiritual beauty. Their pure, upright life, their deep faith and devotion to God, their gentleness and their wonderful manliness became a shining example of real life for many thousands of prisoners. One could see Christ reflected in their faces. I, too, wanted to live just such a pure life with high ideals.

One of the prisoners, a Christian, Nikolai Khrapov, seemed to me to be an especially radiant and incomparable example. I met him in 1953 in one of the camps of Eastern Siberia. Khrapov had been previously sentenced for his faith in God. And now [1970] he is in prison once again. He is fifty-six and of these years he has spent more than half behind prison walls or in camps, just because he is a Christian. He was first of all imprisoned under Stalin, then under Khrushchev and now again under you [i.e. Brezhnev]. He was at liberty only a short time with his family and was then again sentenced to deprivation of liberty.

You must know that many hundreds of Baptists have suffered in this way for years and years – the best sons and daughters of our people. But their bonds and sufferings have turned the attention of many to Christ. The transforming power of Christ and the command of the gospel have subjected not only my heart but the hearts of hundreds like me which had been poisoned by atheism and vice.

The Russian prisons and camps have become for many a place of spiritual regeneration and they have met Christ there. In 1953 I completely broke with my sinful past and with the world of sin. I became a Christian.

There are still thousands of people in the prisons and camps who were like me in the past. They are not being reformed, for the methods of camp education cannot be of any use to them and do not make them better. Indeed, they are becoming worse and worse. They do not need the morality of atheism, they need Christ. If only you did not prevent believers who are even now in the prisons and camps from speaking about Christ to this sinful world! You would not need to maintain your million lecturers upholding atheist morality; you would not need so many police. The money you spend on their maintenance and on waging war against God would be better directed to publishing the Bible and Gospels for our Soviet people. Then there would be fewer drunkards and thieves and less crime; then the camps would significantly empty and you would be able to turn the prisons into museums to human cruelty and savagery, where men were held in concrete cages and hunted like wild animals.

In 1954 I returned from prison and married, but from that moment I began to be persecuted, this time as a believer. In 1961, having by this time five young children, I was sentenced to a year's forced labour for my Christian life. Even before I had served this sentence, I was condemned to five years' exile to Eastern Siberia for my witness to Christ.

I remember my first trial as a Christian in 1961. The public prosecutor wanted to reproach me with a reference to my past. He lifted the big volume of my former convictions high above his head and shaking it, he shouted: 'Look at his past! He was a thief, a gangster, a criminal! And now he has turned into a holy apostle!'

In my defence speech I replied: 'Yes, I was a thief and a criminal, for which I served my sentence deservedly. But now I am dead to sin and to my past. The power of the blood of Christ has cleansed my wicked heart. Now I am a new man. The book that the public prosecutor is waving is now no more than my sinful former self, and it's no good rummaging there to find some balm of comfort for what you're doing.

'Lecturers have been shaking these remains for years now – atheists in their lectures and correspondents in their newspaper articles. . . . Even the President of the Council for Religious Affairs, V. A. Kuroyedov, in the newspaper *Izvestia* (17 October 1969) assiduously tried to resurrect my former sinful self. But Kozlov the criminal and gangster died a long time ago and was buried, while today, by the grace of God, Kozlov the Christian lives.'

Thus began the second stage of my life as a convict; this time not for being a gangster and for robbery, but for Christ. I was taken in a convoy to the Krasnoyarsk territory, but this time I had no feelings of repentance, as in the past. I could already feel the love of Christ and I knew the great commandment that to me, too, 'it was given not only to believe in him, but to suffer for Christ' (Philippians 1: 29). This did console me.

I spent three years in exile, far from my family. My wife and my young children (now six of them) remained without their father, so they, too, experienced the burden of suffering for Christ.

In 1964 I was freed and returned home, but I was not

allowed to remain there long. It was not only at Yoshkar-Ola that the police and other officials could not leave believers in peace, but they were being subjected to reprisals all over the country. As you know, in 1964–5 Baptists from various towns came to Moscow with complaints addressed to different state bodies. In August 1965 more than a hundred representatives appealed to A. I. Mikoyan, President of the Supreme Soviet in Moscow, to receive us and give us a hearing. When assent was received, I was among the five who were received by Mikoyan.

This head of state was presented in a letter with thirty of the most typical facts about lawless and arbitrary treatment of believers. Sixteen pieces of photographic evidence were also presented, showing the destruction of prayer houses, the beating of believers, and so on.

Mikoyan promised to restore freedom of conscience in our country, but in fact, the position of believers did not improve – rather the contrary. I personally was tried again in April 1966 and sentenced to a year's forced labour for my Christian activity. In March 1966 new state decrees were issued with the aim of stepping up the persecution of believers. Local persecution increased.

In May 1966 about five hundred Baptists from one hundred and thirty towns came to Moscow. I was one of them. The believers asked you, Leonid Ilich, to receive us and give us a hearing, as Soviet citizens. But instead of being received, the delegates were thrown into prison cells, into these concrete cages, with varying sentences.

Again I appeared before the court as a Christian. This was the fourth time I had been sentenced for my faith in God. They gave me three years' strict regime. Again my family was left without a father. But we forgave you for all this long ago.

From the very first days of their imprisonment, the believers prayed for you. God heard, so did the gloomy walls of the Lefortovo prison – the main political prison in our country. We prayed for you as our teacher, Christ, in-

95

structed us. He said: 'Bless them that curse you, do good to them that hate you, and pray for them which despitefully use you and persecute you' (Matthew 5: 44). I believe that these prayers which went up day and night will not be in vain.

I was sent to the Arkhangelsk Region to serve my sentence. Hundreds of believers were also subjected to long periods of imprisonment. But the believers who remained at liberty suffered still greater persecutions: the breaking up of meetings, searches and confiscation of religious literature, interrogations, fines, removal of children and trials. . . .

The prisons and the harsh conditions of the labour camps and colonies undermined the health of many believers. Some did not return home. They ended their lives behind barbed wire, as heroes of the faith. But the Christians have forgiven you for this, too. May the tears of fathers and mothers, the tears of orphaned children and the innocent blood of martyred Christians remind you of the greatest evil on earth – the persecution of Christians – and may they melt your hearts.

The time for my release drew near. The local authorities in Yoshkar-Ola told the believers that two days after Kozlov returned home he would be returned to prison.

In August 1969 I was released from camp. From my first day home the police began to call. I started to get summonses to the authorities and to the police. Fines began. In September 1969 I was fined one hundred roubles in a single week for conducting services in my home; a short time later I was again fined one hundred roubles. This was when I was earning seventy roubles a month. My family, my children were sentenced to starvation. The same happened to many families (*Church Times*, 1 January 1971, reprinted as a leaflet entitled *A Criminal becomes a Christian in a Russian Prison*).

For many years there has been no news of Vasili Kozlov.

Whatever his subsequent fate, the influence of such men does not die and the power of his words will live on.

8

'Greater Love Hath No Man'

If there is one characteristic mark of the Christian in the Soviet Union, it is love. The communist system proclaims the brotherhood of man. Yet without belief in the fatherhood of God, Soviet experience shows that there is nothing to root it in real relationships. All too easily the needs of the individual begin to be submerged in the demands of the collective and it is then only a short step to the abolition of the rights of the individual. Class hatred leads eventually to a regime of terror.

For all the slogans in communist newspapers, it can never cease to be a matter of shame to the Soviet authorities that they have not begun to forge the better social relationships which were supposed to be one of the first gains from the Revolution. Christianity, wherever it is found in the USSR, seems at once to demonstrate to those who come into contact with it that it introduces an entirely new dimension of concern into life. Usually Christianity does not need to evangelize; it just needs to be itself.

Because of the mark of love which the Christian carries upon him, what unites the denominations is far more notable than what divides them. In terms of official ecumenical re-lations, Orthodox, Protestants and Catholics in the Soviet Union may be just as far apart as they are in the United States. Yet being received into a community of any of these is to experience life in a micro-environment of love contained within the larger hostile one.

Vasili Kozlov was received into a community of Protestants because it was their influence which he encountered in prison. He might, had his imprisonment been twenty years later and had he been of the opposite sex, have encountered Nijole

Sadunaite, a Roman Catholic, as a prelude to joining the fellowship of the faithful. She, in her turn, happened to be a Catholic because of the chance that she was born a Lithuanian and that was the Church of her people. Lithuanians are as loyal and united in their devotion to their Catholic tradition as are the Poles and they are not losing this unity.

Born in 1939, Nijole Sadunaite missed the short period of freedom her country knew between the two World Wars. Her earliest memories were of the German occupation and her education took place entirely under the new system. The Soviet Union had annexed her country in 1939, then there was a German occupation, followed by the incorporation of all the Baltic States into the Soviet Union at the end of the Second World War.

Nijole has spent six recent years of her life in prison and exile. Arrest and sentence have made only a marginal difference to her goal in life: she has become even more dedicated to her ideal of serving others. Even before her imprisonment she never seems to have thought of herself. Nijole dedicated her life to nursing sick clergy and to promoting the cause of freedom for the Church in whose truths she believed so passionately. She helped to produce and circulate a journal devoted to this cause: the *Chronicle of the Lithuanian Catholic Church*. Typed in secret, it was circulated more or less openly and every one of the fifty issues since it first came out in March 1972 has reached us at Keston College with the instruction, implicit or explicit: 'Make all these facts known to the world.' The KGB found a half-finished copy on Nijole's typewriter when they arrested her.

Friends managed somehow to pass through the KGB cordons and witness her trial in June 1975.[1] From their record, we know how Nijole Sadunaite defended herself. Far from being intimidated by her accusers, she used the dock of the courtroom as though it were the pulpit of a church. Her

[1] For a fuller account of Nijole's trial, *see* Michael Bourdeaux, *Land of Crosses*, 1979, pp. 282–8.

congregation was her prosecutor, the judge, and the assembled rows of hostile, hand-picked atheists, workers given a day off to go and jeer at this defenceless young woman. Turning to her accusers, she said: 'I love you all as if you were my brothers and sisters; I wouldn't hesitate to give my life for any one of you. Today you don't need my sacrifice, though. What you do need is to hear the truth spoken to your faces. This *Lithuanian Chronicle* is like a mirror which reflects all the crimes of the atheists against those who believe in God. Nothing evil likes to look at its own image, it hates its own reflection. That's why you hate everyone who tears off the veil of falsehood and hypocrisy behind which you're hiding.'

On hearing her sentence of six years' labour-camp and exile, Nijole said: 'This is the happiest day of my life. Today I stand beside eternal truth, beside the person of Jesus Christ. How can I fail to be happy when Almighty God has already shown that light triumphs over darkness and truth over lies and falsehood?'

But really this was the beginning, not the end of her story. It is truly remarkable how religious believers – and for that matter other fearless activists in the cause of human rights – manage to communicate from within their prisons. Page after page of subsequent issues of the *Lithuanian Chronicle* testify not only to Nijole's goodness, but to its effect on the most depraved sectors of Soviet society with whom she was thrown into bodily contact. Having just survived a four-week journey to the camp, deprived of even the most basic necessities of life, locked in an iron cage, she was almost too weak to work. Periods in the camp hospital alternated with spells of forced labour. In a primitive glass-cutting workshop without the benefit of even the most basic safety regulations, her nose and lungs were assaulted by a constant cloud of noxious dust. She was too weak to work a lathe, so the guards forced her to produce gloves. Her norm was seventy pairs a day, six days a week, no excuses accepted for failing. To fulfil it she had to work from six in the morning until ten at night. Yet she could still write:

How good it is that the small craft of my life is being steered by the hand of the good Father. When he is at the helm nothing is to be feared. Then, no matter how difficult life may be, you will know how to resist and love. I can say that the year 1975 has flown by like a flash, it has been a year of joy for me. I thank the good Lord for it. . . .

We have many old women and sick people, so I rejoice that I have been brought here in accordance with my calling – to nurse and to love. Although I long greatly to see you all, it will be hard for me to leave here. It will be distressing to leave people who have become so near and dear to me, but the good Lord does indeed care for us most of all. . . .

I receive letters not only from acquaintances, but also from some whom I have never met. I am so moved by people's desire to help in any way possible. How much feeling and sincerity there is in people's hearts. How encouraging is all this, how it raises one's spirit and stimulates one to be better, to be worthy of such great love.

Nijole Sadunaite survived numerous bouts of ill health in prison in Mordovia to reach the end of that part of her sentence in 1977. In March that year all the letters which had somehow come through to her were confiscated. She was summoned for interrogation and promised that she could go straight home to Lithuania if she would renounce her activities. She rejected this temptation out of hand, despite threats that her exile could be made a hundred times more difficult. 'The more difficult the better', she replied.

At this time the KGB photographed her in her civilian clothes, which she had not been able to wear for years, to show how 'well' she was looking and they circulated these pictures abroad.

Now Nijole had to face a gruelling rail journey of twenty-seven days in crowded prison wagons, all the way from European Russia, where she had been imprisoned; to Boguchany, the place of her Siberian exile.[2] The train made many stops to drop or pick up prisoners. Even in these appalling conditions she managed to retain her sense of humour. In a letter home she described the unhygienic conditions thus:

> By a stroke of luck I did not get any lice. However, I had to fight off bedbugs with all my might, and the other women – more accustomed to them – were able to laugh heartily at my efforts. Alas, I have not learned to sleep when the bugs are biting . . . and if I miss sleep for a night or two, the last of my strength goes. It is not surprising that my heart went on strike. . . . On 5 September I almost journeyed to the place where there is no pain and no tears – what was most interesting was that I felt quite calm – no fear. I had only the one clear thought: thank God, everything is ending.

However, at this point, the guards administered some emergency medical treatment, and she recovered, although she continued to suffer from flu and inflammation of the ears for the rest of the journey . . .

> I have one partially deaf ear as a reminder. . . . Thanks be to the good Lord, I can hear with the other. It would be nice if I were incapable of hearing all the cursing and filthy language and could enjoy only the sound of good words and the varied musical tones of nature.

On reaching Boguchany, Nijole was given work as a cleaner in the local school. She and another woman had to wash all the rooms daily, but in spite of the hard work she felt herself recovering:

> Ten days of freedom and now I stand firmly on my feet and no longer fear a strong wind. The weakness is passing off, I get less tired and I feel that I shall very soon be as

[2] For this description of Nijole's journey into exile, I am indebted to *Keston News Service* 53, 15 June 1978, which I quote verbatim.

strong as I was before. . . . They have still not sent me my money from the camp. If it had not been for good people I would have had to go hungry. I get on well with the people here. All are friendly and good to me. I'll try not to remain in their debt. . . . I breathe the pure air of the *taiga* deep into my lungs and rejoice in the wide open spaces. . . . Thank you, good Lord, for that beauty in nature, for the sparks of goodness in people's souls.

However, after Nijole had spent only three months in Boguchany, the authorities apparently felt that she was too comfortably placed there: some friends from Lithuania had managed to visit her. She was told she would be transferred to the even more remote village of Irba, one hundred kilometres from Boguchany, on 20 December 1977. It is a broken-down collective farm, notorious throughout the district, which can be reached only by aeroplane three times a week. However, before she could be sent off, Nijole was sent to hospital with high temperature and intestinal pains. TB was suspected, but it turned out to be chronic inflammation of the gall-bladder. She was discharged in January 1978.

During her exile Nijole received many letters from abroad, from the USA, England, Norway, West Germany, Poland and other countries. She even received some parcels. She mentions especially a letter sent to her by the girls of the Verona Lyceum in Italy, encouraging her and assuring her of their prayers and support. She writes, 'To all who remember me – my heartfelt thanks! May the good Lord bless and protect them all!'

This is not to say that the food parcels from abroad always reached her safely. The *Lithuanian Chronicle* (No. 41, from which this account is taken) contains a detailed description of the violence done to the parcels and the personal harassment of Nijole which resulted, a series of scenes which would be farcical if they were not so sad. An extract from the *Chronicle* reads:

Medical doctor W. Barenberg from West Germany in-

cluded some cheese in a package. The customs agents replaced the cheese with a document stating they had burned
it.

Doctor of Philosophy and Theology Lilly Zarncke sent
powdered milk from West Germany; the customs officials
again inserted a note that they had burned the milk. Nijole
writes: 'The list of "forbidden" food products is growing.
I recently received honey in three parcels, but now even
this is being confiscated. Many of the food products sent
me are confiscated, often without proper documentation.
The list of contents is removed from packages to facilitate
theft.'

Customs officials destroy some of the parcels. Nijole
writes: 'A parcel came from Austria: it was all torn, the
cocoa was spilled, the parcel looked as if it had gone
through a bomb attack.'

'Whatever food I have left, I distribute to all political
exiles, regardless of their nationality. Even were a person
of really bad will in trouble, I would share with him my
last morsel of bread, for we have been told to do this by
our good master, Jesus Christ', writes Nijole from Boguchany. Her personal needs are very small – she distributes
and passes on nearly everything to those who are suffering.
That is probably why KGB customs officials plunder Nijole's packages and parcels to such an extent.

On 22 June 1979 Nijole Sadunaite wrote a statement to
the head of the Internal Affairs Department of the Boguchany district, requesting permission to travel to Vilnius to
visit her family during her vacation in August. On 4 July
a militia employee informed Nijole that she was denied
permission to go to Vilnius during her vacation and would
be forbidden to do so in the future. Under Soviet law, all
exiles have the right to spend ten days in their homeland.
'The security agents made me very happy', writes Nijole,
'when they said that even were I exiled for ten years, they
would not allow me to take a single vacation. It means that
Lithuania is alive. The security police fear us.'

In a letter which she was able to write during her exile, Nijole remembers some of the girls who had become her friends and whom she had had to leave behind in the prison camp. She, a Catholic, writes with especial warmth of a Russian Orthodox girl she had befriended:

Nadya Usoeva is a girl of remarkable goodness and tact (sentenced to seven years of strict-regime labour camp and two[3] years of exile). She is a very decent and high-minded Russian Orthodox girl. We were like sisters, only unfortunately she was hardly ever permitted to 'take a holiday' at the labour camp. It is a real miracle: where does that fragile girl get her strength? Five years of punishment cell and strict-regime prison with hardly a break – starvation, cold and ridicule. She is a true heroine before whom we should all kneel. Quiet, calm, always smiling, with a prayer on her lips. I never heard her utter an impatient or rough word. She goes to the punishment cell smiling and returns smiling. Exhausted, blue with cold, she looks terrible, yet smiles not only at us, but at her tormentors as well. Her example used to move me to tears and it still does. Please write to her yourselves occasionally. She will then be at least partially rewarded for the constant brutality and ridicule she endures. Lord, how much suffering and injustice is in this valley of tears!

Nijole also writes of people she had been close to earlier in her life. Of Canon Petras Rauda, whom she had nursed as an old man during his terminal illness, she says:

The finest of his characteristics was love of humanity, forgiveness and deep faith. I will never forget his last days of living on earth. Although suffering great pain, he refused any drugs to lessen it, in atonement for our fellow-country-

[3] Five years of exile, according to *Russkaya Mysl*, 25 August 1977. The same source says she was formerly a medical student, before being sentenced for her activities as a member of the group called the 'True Orthodox Christians'. The last news of her (1979) was that she had begun her exile.

men who had gone astray. He was at peace and serene, but also grateful for the least service – a man of amazing sensitivity and beauty.

Friends who came to visit him could not bear it and began to weep, but the Monsignor calmly and convincingly told them: 'Don't cry, for I'm going to the good Father. . . .'

The university of life – prisons, trips to labour camps (God save even enemies from such 'trips'!) and exile – all the more clearly and distinctly illuminated reality and what man becomes when he loses faith in God. Without their masks, our fine-talking 'humanists' appeared in their true light with regard to myself and thousands of the best of the best. Therefore nothing now amazes me; it only remains for me to pray for them. Their cruelty and hatred merely bring into sharper focus the nobility and moral beauty of the innocent guilty.

Nijole was indeed an amazing letter-writer. Probably only a tiny proportion of what she wrote has penetrated to us in the West, or even reached the friends in Lithuania and elsewhere in the USSR to whom she addressed them. The *Chronicle* (No. 39) talks of her averaging twenty to thirty letters on every one of her days off during her exile. On one day she even managed thirty-seven. Here indeed is a rich spiritual harvest, the surviving ones deserving editing and publication, with the promise that one day they will belong to the corpus of spiritual classics of the twentieth century.

On 8 July 1980 Nijole was released from exile and received permission to fly home to Vilnius via Riga. At Riga airport she was taken off the plane by three KGB men, who pushed her into a car and drove her to Vilnius (a five-hour journey). This was done to prevent 'welcoming committees' meeting Nijole at Riga and Vilnius airports and publicly giving her flowers. Some of the would-be welcomers were detained by the KGB.

The news of her return was broadcast on foreign radio stations and many people came to see her to thank her personally for her self-sacrifice. Nijole told them: 'Thank you all for your prayers and support. It was only because of your prayers that I have been able to bear it all.'

She has tried to write and thank her friends abroad who had sent her parcels or letters, but the KGB is now confiscating all replies or presents sent to her.

A friend, Gemma-Jadwyga Stanelyte, who visited Nijole in Siberia, was sentenced in December 1980 to three years in the camps for organizing a religious procession.

In the summer of 1981, Nijole was even visited by friends from abroad, who found that she was still radiating the qualities which had illuminated her personality during the whole of her imprisonment and exile. Heedless of the danger, while under constant observation by the KGB, she was determined to do anything and everything to which her faith led her. Clearly, danger of future imprisonment faces her daily. Clearly, too, any single day of her life over the last ten years marks her out for future sainthood in her Church. 'Greater love hath no man' than Nijole has shown to friends, fellow-prisoners and persecutors alike.

Epilogue

'Within the mass of the world's vastest country there is such
a diversity of race, culture and language that the existence of
pluralism is scarcely surprising. Here and there non-conform-
ing elements exist, especially related to nationalist aspirations,
though they should not be unduly emphasized. After all,
Soviet control works in a kind of way, even in Poland. The
major alternative to capitalism will continue to be Marxism.
The continued existence of Christianity, Judaism and, in its
own areas, Islam, even signs of religious revival here and
there, do not seriously distort the above generalization.'

This is my own summary of attitudes I have heard recently
expressed by intelligent people who know something about
the Soviet scene. I happen to disagree profoundly with this
view.

Stalinism delivered a body-blow to Marxism, in my
opinion, from which it will not recover. Present harsh policies
towards non-conformists, be they internal to 'Helsinki moni-
tors' or external to Polish Solidarity activists, are the thrash-
ings of death-agony rather than determined surges of inward
strength.

Therefore what is contained in this book has a political as
well as a religious significance. Upon the ruins of Soviet
ideology something one day will be rebuilt. No one can yet
forecast what that will be. Nationalism could in certain areas
become explosive enough to force change, but by its very
nature it is divisive among the many peoples who inhabit the
Soviet Union. Christianity does not overtly contain as much
power, yet its inner strength is more cohesive. Furthermore,
even though it is sometimes linked with nationalism (for ex-

ample, the Russian Orthodox Church or the Catholic Church in Lithuania) it has the power at the same time often to transcend such considerations.

It is already certain that, whatever else the twenty-first century may bring to the Soviet Union, Christianity will be a formative influence, perhaps more so than is yet surmised, even by those with inside knowledge. While the Soviet Union, like Poland, is a great refrigerator of religious conservatism, with Protestants, Catholics and Orthodox demonstrating that a church does not have to embrace 'modernism' to retain a hold on the human heart, at the same time there are signs of a great yearning here and there for Christian unity.

This book has itself illustrated this in places. It is ironical that the longing for unity is entirely outside and unrecognized by any official movement. Indeed, those in the USSR who most long for unity are barred from any ecumenical meeting. Those who would most benefit from contacts with foreigners – and there is no Soviet-based ecumenical movement – are kept away from them.

It hardly needs stressing that if real Christian unity should make strides in the Soviet Union, this would be something of immense significance for the future, both of that country and of the world. Perhaps God is saying to the Church today that Christians in comfortable democracies cannot stir themselves to come together, while under pressure the need for unity is that much more urgent.

The reader of this book will realize that we are not totally in the realm of fantasy at this point. Perhaps the indications are isolated and add up to nothing resembling a complete picture. Yet every movement has a beginning and the idea of the ten thousand who did not bow the knee to Baal, the brand plucked from the burning, the disciples, the *ecclesia* is central to the message of the Bible.

No two Christian groups are further from each other in the Soviet Union than the Orthodox and the Pentecostals. Yet when Father Gleb Yakunin was arrested, a group of Pentecostals wrote a petition in support of him, a moving recognition of his earlier championing of their cause when they were in such deep trouble.

Father Dmitri Dudko, an Orthodox youth leader and preacher, holds up a conversion to the Baptist faith from atheism as something admirable (p. 90). Anatoli Levitin, in total isolation in a Soviet prison, calls before him a panorama of the *oikumene* as though it were a slide-show, suffuses his prayers for all churches everywhere with an intensity of longing and devotion (p. 59).

In 1982 the mother of Galina Vilchinskaya, a 23–year–old Baptist girl from Brest, Belorussia, now in a Siberian prison camp, wrote:

> Galina is able to have fellowship with a woman of Russian Orthodox background. She is 52, a language teacher fluent in four languages. She is very upright and one who loves the Lord from the bottom of her heart. This unites her with Galina. They pray together and share with one another the few things they have at their disposal.

Nowhere is this longing for unity more to the fore than with the Christian Seminar in Moscow. Earlier (pp. 30–35) I described some of its activities before it was broken up by the KGB. Its ideas are recounted movingly by Philip Walters in an article in *Religion in Communist Lands* (Vol. 9, Nos. 3–4, Autumn 1981, pp. 111–126).

The group was seeking to establish a new kind of Christian community, based on respect, integrity, unity, New Testament ideals. In particular, it wanted to rediscover the practical reality of the old Orthodox ideal of 'sobornost'. As Dr Walters says:

> It is Christian love which creates the 'community' and binds it together: and an essential element in Christian love is freedom. The paradoxical combination of individual liberty and free unity constitutes the essence of *sobornost*, which receives such development in Russian Orthodox theology: and the *community* of the Seminar is seen by its members as

an example of *sobornost* at work. 'Do not imagine', say Seminar members, 'that we have exchanged the totalitarianism of communist ideology for the totalitarianism of ecclesiastical legalism (. . .) In this divided world we are trying to produce a community as the "unity of the spirit in the bond of peace" (. . .) It is not in isolated self-assertion, even if this involves creative activity, that we find the depths of our personality, but in fraternal love in the image of the Holy Trinity (. . .)

The desire for unity with other Christians, both inside and outside the Soviet Union, was pressing and urgent, but was devastatingly interrupted by direct police intervention. During the preceding years the Seminar was most successful in establishing contact with young Italian Catholics. The relationship with a renewal movement, *Communione e Liberazione*, developed in a specially warm and personal way. Is it too much to hope that a Slav Pope may yet have some unforeseen influence?

Christian renewal walks half a pace ahead of this desire for unity. Nowhere in this book is the renewal more tellingly described than in the words of Alexander Ogorodnikov and Boris Razveyev to Philip Potter, General Secretary of the WCC (pp. 47–48). Or, in the words of Anatoli Levitin (p. 28): 'Life is beginning to stir. What will the day be like?'

So for the Soviet Union Christianity will play a role in the shaping of the society of the twenty-first century. There is nowhere else in the world where belief shows such intensity, having been formed in the crucible of suffering. Soviet Christians live very close to the spirit of the New Testament. In them one day the world will rediscover the courage of uncompromising belief it has lost.

Finally, salvation is seen to be at work in our generation. Miracles of faith are worked daily. The kingdom of heaven is at hand.

111

Bibliography

(Except where otherwise indicated, place of publication is London)

Books

Bourdeaux, M. A., *Faith on Trial in Russia*, Keston Book No. 1. Hodder & Stoughton, 1971.

—, *Patriarch & Prophets*, Keston Book No. 2. Mowbrays, 1975.

—, *Opium of the People*, Keston Boook No. 9. 2nd ed., Mowbrays, 1977.

—, *Land of Crosses, the Struggle for Religious Freedom in Lithuania 1939–1978*. Chulmleigh, Devon, Augustine Publishing Co., 1979.

Dudko, Fr. D., *Our Hope*. New York, St. Vladimir's Seminary Press, 1977.

Gerodnik, G., *The Truth about the Monastery of the Caves at Pskov (Pravda o Pskovo-Pechorskom Monastyre)*. Moscow, Politicheskaya Literature, 1963.

Ginzburg, E., *Into the Whirlwind*. Collins–Harvill, 1967.

Nikon, Fr., *Letters to my Spiritual Children*, published in Russian. Paris, YMCA Press, 1979.

Sapiets, M. tr., *The Unknown Homeland*, Keston Book No. 13. Mowbrays, 1978.

Solzhenitsyn, A., *The Gulag Archipelago*. Collins–Harvill, Vol. I 1974, Vol. II 1975, Vol. III 1978.

—, *August 1914*. Bodley Head, 1972.

—, *One Day in the Life of Ivan Denisovich*. Penguin, 1963.

—, ed., *From Under the Rubble* (collection of essays). Collins–Harvill, 1975.

Report

Religious Liberty in the Soviet Union: World Council of Churches and USSR, post-Nairobi documentation. M. Bourdeaux, H. Hebly, E. Voss eds. Keston College, Heathfield Road, Keston, Kent.

112

Journals

Religion in Communist Lands, Keston College journal, now published tri-annually.

Keston News Service, Keston College bi-monthly information bulletin.

Glaube in der 2 Welt, Journal on Religion, Atheism and Human Rights, Institute of *Glaube in der 2 Welt*, Zollikon, Switzerland.

Nadezhda (Hope) (*samizdat* journal), Frankfurt, Possev, published bi-annually.

Russia Cristiana, Milan, Centro Studi Russia Cristiana, published bi-monthly.

Russkaya Mysl (*La Pensée Russe*), Russian *émigré* weekly newspaper, published in Paris.

Journal of the Moscow Patriarchate, Official Journal of the Russian Orthodox Church, Moscow, published monthly.